A TRUTH
versus
THE TRUTH

How Religious People Embrace
or Resist the Modern World

*A Guide to Recognizing and
Talking About Faith in Everyday Life*

STEPHEN B. ROBERTS

Next Steps Publishing

Copyright © 2025 by Stephen B. Roberts

All rights reserved. No part of this book may be reproduced, stored in a retrieval system, or transmitted in any form or by any means—electronic, mechanical, photocopying, recording, or otherwise—without the prior written permission of the publisher, except in the case of brief quotations embodied in critical articles or reviews. This publication may not be used in whole or in part for the development, training, or enhancement of artificial intelligence (AI) or machine learning (ML) technologies without the express written consent of the author and publisher.

This book is a work of nonfiction. While every effort has been made to ensure accuracy, the author and publisher disclaim liability for any errors or omissions. The views expressed are those of the author and do not necessarily reflect those of the publisher or any affiliated organizations.

Published by: Next Steps Publishing
Red Hook, NY
For information, permissions, or bulk orders, contact:
Next Steps Publishing: Info@nextstepspublishing.net
ISBN 979-8-9993880-0-1 (hardcover)
979-8-9993880-1-8 (epub)
First Edition
Printed in the United States of America

To my siblings—David, Jonathan, Mark, Scott, and Pam—and to my first cousins—Sue, Bruce, Todd, and Cynthia—whose shared stories of our upbringing offered deep insight and understanding that helped shape this manuscript.

To REH—without your unwavering support, this manuscript would never have been completed, let alone begun.

To JH—with heartfelt thanks for your many years of steadfast guidance.

Contents

1. General Introduction — 1
2. Marker 1: "A" Truth versus "The" Truth — 25
3. Marker 2: Violence Regarding "The Other" and Purity Within — 40
4. Marker 3: Physical and Social Isolation — 59
5. Marker 4: Modesty: Dress, Clothing, and Physical Contact — 69
6. Marker 5: Science and Technology — 80
7. Marker 6: Education — 95
8. Marker 7: Language — 113
9. Marker 8: Food and Drink — 123
10. Marker 9: Treatment of Women — 134

11. Marker 10: Sex, Gender, and Sexuality   159

CHAPTER ONE

GENERAL INTRODUCTION

A few years ago, I was asked to speak about cooperation and tolerance among Judaism, Islam, and Christianity. The topic was close to my heart. Throughout my career, I have worked closely with people of different faiths. I have seen how much we share and also how much divides us.

I am a rabbi. Since I was ordained, I have worked as a professional chaplain in healthcare and disaster settings. A chaplain is a clergy member of any faith who helps people during difficult times. Chaplains work in places like hospitals, prisons, and nursing homes. We provide support when people are sick, grieving, or in crisis. We listen, comfort, and help people find strength in their own beliefs.

One of the most unique things about being a chaplain is working with people of all faiths. I help people when they are feeling lost, scared, or in pain. I meet them where they are. I help them find strength in their own beliefs. I listen as they share thoughts about God, rituals, and what happens after death. Every day for the past 30 years, I have worked with both Jews and non-Jews, helping them with life's biggest questions.

Over the years, I have learned that most people of faith are open to working with others. But not all. Some people resist cooperation. They prefer to stay within their own religious group and reject those who are different. I have spent many years trying to understand why. What makes some people open, and others closed?

The Modernity Spectrum

The goals of this book are simple. First, to create a new taxonomy—meaning a clear way to group and describe things—that I call the *Modernity Spectrum*. It helps us look at how people of faith either accept or resist the modern world. The Modernity Spectrum works for all religious traditions.

Second, to create a tool to help stop "othering." The Modernity Spectrum is that tool: it gives us a fair way to talk about how people live their faith. It uses Ten Markers —also called Identifiers, discussed below—to help us understand where someone falls on the Modernity Spectrum.

The Modernity Spectrum Defined

All faith traditions can be found somewhere on the **Modernity Spectrum**.

- At one end is the **Modern side**. People here practice their faith in ways that fit well with today's world. They use new technology, send their kids to public schools, and are part of everyday life. When I say "modern," I mean people who accept science, believe in personal choice, and live in open and mixed communities. The rest of this book will explain what "modern" means when it comes to faith and religion.

- At the other end is the **Non-Modern side**. People here try to live apart from today's world. They may reject new technology. Some live in small communities—sometimes in cities, sometimes far away. They may dress in ways that show they don't follow modern trends. Their choices often send a message: *"I do not want to be part of today's world."*

The Modernity Spectrum helps us understand how religious people respond to modern life. Some embrace it. Others resist it. Most fall somewhere in between.

This divide exists in every religion. Many people live their faith while participating in modern society. Others reject modern influences and try to remain separate.

No group is 100% modern or 100% non-modern. Most are a mix of both. The purpose of the Modernity Spectrum is to help find where a group falls between the two ends.

The Modernity Spectrum gives us a shared way to talk about this difference. No matter where we live, what language we speak, or how much education we have, this tool can help us describe how people live their faith. It works like a checklist—clear, simple, and based on facts.

It also allows us to compare religious life across traditions. Sometimes, people from different religions have more in common—based on where they fall on the Modernity Spectrum—than they do with others in their own faith.

Think of it this way:

Modern. Non-Modern.

Two clear terms. These help replace older words that are often misunderstood or used differently by different groups. These older terms—like those in the list below—can confuse more than they help. They don't let us compare faith practices clearly or fairly across traditions.

Here are just a few of those confusing terms:
- Reform

- Conservative

- Orthodox
- Ultra-Orthodox
- Fundamentalist
- Traditional
- Progressive
- Evangelical
- Literalist
- Liberal
- Extremist
- Mainstream

Faith can bring people together or pull them apart. It can be used to heal—or to harm. This is true in every tradition.

If we want people of faith to work together, we need to start by understanding our own traditions. We also need to stop "othering" people from different traditions.

What is "othering"—and why is it so harmful?

Othering

Othering means treating people like they don't belong. It happens when some people are seen as "normal" and others are seen as different, strange, or wrong. People who are "othered" are often pushed outside of the main group. They are made to feel like they are not part of "us."

Othering can happen because of race, religion, language, gender, or where someone is from. It can also be based on how someone looks, dresses, or lives. When we other someone, we say, "They are not like me," or "They are not one of us." This kind of thinking separates people instead of bringing them together.

Othering is not just about seeing someone as different. It often means thinking badly of them because of that difference. It can, and often does, lead to unfair treatment or hurtful actions. People who are othered may be treated as if they are less important or less human.

On a small level, othering causes bullying or unfair judgment. On a bigger level, it can lead to whole groups being mistreated. Some groups may be denied basic rights. In some cases, othering has even led to violence, war, or genocide.

Othering takes away people's dignity. It says that some lives matter less than others. That can be very dangerous.

The opposite of othering is belonging. Belonging means people are included and accepted for who they are. It means everyone has value and deserves to be treated with kindness and respect.

Every Religion Has Both Modern and Non-Modern Followers

No one faith has a monopoly on extremism. Yet, those who other people often believe—and say—the opposite. They claim something like: "No one of my faith tradition would ever do or say X, Y, Z."

The truth is very different. Every religion has both modern and non-modern followers. And the more non-modern the outlook, often the more extreme the behavior. This is not unique to any one religion, though it is commonly portrayed that way. For example, some ultra-Orthodox (ultra non-modern on the Modernity Spectrum) Jewish men in Israel throw rocks at cars on the

Sabbath. Some have even assassinated leaders, encouraged by extremist rabbis. When I recognize and acknowledge the problems in my own tradition, it also helps me to see them in others. This can be a strong antidote to othering.

- For every modern rabbi who teaches respect, we have a non-modern one who spreads intolerance.

- For every modern Christian who builds interfaith bridges, we have a non-modern one who burns crosses.

- For every peaceful modern Buddhist monk, we have non-modern extremists who incite violence, like those in Myanmar.

- For every modern Hindu guru, we have a non-modern caste-system enforcer.

- For every modern Muslim leader who preaches peace, we have a non-modern one who calls for violence.

- For every modern evangelical pastor, we have a non-modern cult leader like David Koresh or Jim Jones.

There are those who say their religion is the only true way. They believe they must separate from the modern world to stay pure. Others believe faith should grow and change with the times. They embrace progress while holding onto tradition. Neither approach is all right or all wrong. But when faith is used to harm, exclude, or attack others, it loses its purpose.

When we Honestly Look at our own Faiths, we can Open our Hearts to Others

When we listen to those who practice differently, we can learn from them. That is how we build cooperation and tolerance.

I have seen firsthand how faith communities can work together. In hospitals, chaplains from different religions support the same patients. In disaster zones, religious leaders from different backgrounds come together to help those in need. When we focus on our shared values—kindness, compassion, and justice—we can accomplish great things.

But this work requires effort. It requires us to step outside our comfort zones. It requires us to challenge our own assumptions. It requires us to listen.

I look forward to learning more from you, the reader. Together, we can build a world where people of all faiths respect and support one another. A world where cooperation is stronger than division. A world where tolerance is not just a word, but a way of life.

The Ten Markers that Make up the Modernity Spectrum

These ten markers of the Modernity Spectrum are universal. That means they work for every religion. They help us compare religious practice, not just within one religion, but across all religions. Sometimes, a person shares more beliefs and daily practices of values with someone from a different religion than with someone from their own. These markers help us see that.

Taken together, the markers give us a simple but powerful way to look at how open or closed a faith group is to the modern world. They help us start better conversations about religion and belief in daily life. They help us ask better questions, see patterns, and understand others more clearly.

- The Modernity Spectrum helps us see how people live out their faith—no matter what religion they follow.

- The ten markers give us a fair and simple way to talk about religion without putting others down.

- The Modernity Spectrum helps us find shared values with people from other faiths—even those who believe differently.

- It gives us words to talk about religious practice that are clearer than labels like "Orthodox" or "liberal."

- Most of all, it helps us build respect across faith traditions instead of walls between them.

Here is a list of the ten **Markers**, or identifiers:

1. **"A" Truth versus "The" Truth**

2. **Violence Regarding "The Other" and Purity Within**

3. **Physical and Social Isolation**

4. **Modesty: Dress, Clothing, and Physical Contact**

5. **Science and Technology**

6. **Education**

7. **Language (e.g., Yiddish, Pennsylvania Dutch)**

8. **Food and Drink**

9. **Treatment of Women**

10. **Sex, Gender, and Sexuality**

What follows is a brief introduction to each of the ten markers/identifiers. The rest of the book will then examine each one in detail.

Marker 1: "A" Truth versus "The" Truth

Some people believe their faith is the only true path. Others believe their faith is true for them but respect other beliefs. The more someone thinks they have "the one and only truth," the less likely they are to accept others. This kind of thinking often leads to conflict, even within the same religion. People can be most harsh toward those who share their faith but practice it differently.

This issue is not unique to any one faith. There have been conflicts within Christianity, Islam, and Judaism over different interpretations of religious teachings. These internal divisions can be just as strong as the ones between different religions. Some disagreements lead to arguments, while others divide entire communities. Families have split apart over differences in belief. Friends have stopped speaking to one another. Wars have been fought. The question we must ask ourselves is whether we can respect those who believe differently, even within our own faith tradition.

Marker 2: Violence Regarding "The Other" and Purity Within

Some religious groups use violence to enforce religious laws or protect purity. Extremists in various traditions have attacked those who do not conform to their beliefs. They may see outsiders as a threat or view those who break religious rules as dangerous to the community. Violence can take many forms. It can be physical, such as attacks or punishments, or social, such as shunning and exclusion.

While most religious people reject violence, some groups justify it as a way to defend their faith. They may believe that protecting their beliefs requires action, even if it harms others. Understanding how different traditions approach this issue helps us see where they fall on the Modernity Spectrum. Groups that reject violence in favor of dialogue and cooperation tend to be more modern. Those that rely on force or punishment to maintain religious purity tend to be more non-modern.

Marker 3: Physical and Social Isolation

Some faith groups isolate themselves from the larger world. They create religious enclaves where they interact only with their own. These groups may limit outside influences by controlling education, banning certain books, or restricting access to media and technology. They may avoid contact with those who do not share their beliefs. Physical isolation is often seen as a way to protect religious values and traditions.

Other groups encourage engagement with different communities. They believe faith can exist alongside modern life. They do not see outside influences as a threat. Instead, they see them as opportunities to grow, learn, and share their beliefs. Whether a group isolates itself or interacts with others can tell us a lot about where they fall on the Modernity Spectrum.

Marker 4: Modesty: Dress, Clothing, and Physical Contact

Many religious traditions have strict rules about modesty, especially for women. If you put a woman from Western

Turkey, an ultra-Orthodox Jewish woman from *Mea Shearim* (an isolated Jewish community in Jerusalem), an Amish woman, and a woman from a small Christian church in Appalachia in the same room, you might think they belong to the same religion. They all cover their hair, arms, and legs in similar ways.

Modesty rules often reflect a group's beliefs about morality and purity. Some communities believe covering the body shows respect for God and tradition. Others see modest dress as a way to separate themselves from the outside world. In contrast, some faith traditions do not focus on modest dress at all. They believe that clothing is a personal choice and that faith is shown through actions, not appearance.

Some communities, out of a strong religious belief in modesty, do not touch people of the opposite sex who are not immediate family members. This includes things like handshakes, hugs, or even passing an object directly from hand to hand. In these communities, touch is seen as something sacred or private, and it is often reserved for close family or spouses only. The rules are not just about actions—they are about respect, boundaries, and keeping focus on spiritual values.

In some cases, these modesty rules go beyond touch. They include rules about looking at others. For example, in certain ultra-Orthodox Jewish or conservative Muslim communities, men and women may avoid making direct eye contact with the opposite sex. This is not meant to be rude. It is seen as a way to protect both people from inappropriate thoughts and feelings. Looking too long or too directly may be viewed as a form of intimacy.

Marker 5: Science and Technology

Some faith groups reject modern science and technology. The Amish, for example, use horse-drawn buggies instead of cars. They avoid modern inventions like zippers. Some religious communities reject television and the internet. They fear that too much contact with the outside world will weaken their beliefs. Others reject medical advancements, choosing faith healing over doctors and hospitals.

Other religious groups fully embrace science. They see no conflict between faith and progress. They welcome modern medicine, scientific discoveries, and technological advancements. Many religious leaders encourage their followers to seek education and use modern tools to improve their communities. Some even argue that science and religion can work together, helping us understand both the physical and spiritual worlds.

Marker 6: Education

Some religious groups encourage learning, science, and philosophy. They believe that knowledge strengthens faith. They see education as a way to explore the world and better understand religious teachings. Many religious schools teach a wide range of subjects, from history and literature to math and science. Some faith traditions even encourage higher education and academic study.

Other groups fear that secular education will weaken faith. They limit what their children can learn, restricting subjects like evolution, philosophy, or history. They may only allow religious texts to be studied. Some communities discourage higher education altogether, believing it leads people away from their faith. The way a religious group approaches education can tell us a lot about where they fall on the Modernity Spectrum.

Marker 7: Languages (Yiddish, Pennsylvania Dutch)

Some religious communities maintain unique languages, such as Yiddish or Pennsylvania Dutch, to preserve their traditions and separate themselves from the broader world. Ritual language, such as using Latin for the Catholic mass, can also be an example of this. Arabic, for instance, is used in Muslim prayer around the world, even by people who speak other languages at home. In Hindu communities, Sanskrit is still used in some ceremonies, even though most people speak local languages in daily life. Language can serve as a connection to the past, linking a community to its ancestors. It can also create a barrier, making it harder for outsiders to join or understand the group.

Some communities insist on speaking only their religious language in daily life, avoiding the language of the broader society. Others use both their traditional language and a modern language, depending on the setting. Language can be a powerful tool for connection but also for isolation.

Marker 8: Food and Drink

Food rules can also show where someone falls on the Modernity Spectrum. Some follow strict dietary laws that separate them from others. Kosher and halal laws, for example, dictate what foods can be eaten and how they must be prepared. Some religious groups avoid alcohol, caffeine, or certain meats.

Other groups take a more flexible approach. They may follow some food restrictions but find ways to eat with those who do not share their faith. In many cultures, sharing a meal is an important way to build relationships, but food restrictions can sometimes create barriers between different groups.

Marker 9: Treatment of Women

Different faith traditions have varying roles for women. Some allow full participation in religious life, including leadership roles. Women can serve as clergy, lead prayers, and make religious decisions. Others limit women's roles, restricting them from leadership or requiring them to follow strict gender roles.

Some traditions encourage women to seek education and careers. Others expect them to focus on family and home life. The way a religious group treats women can tell us a lot about where they fall on the Modernity Spectrum. Groups that allow equal participation tend to be more modern, while those that limit women's roles tend to be more non-modern.

Marker 10: Sex, Gender, and Sexuality

Religions and people of faith have different beliefs about sex, gender, and sexuality. What a person of faith believes about sex, gender, and sexuality can often shape how and who they connect with in the world of today.

One reason the Modernity Spectrum has many elements on it is that someone's views might cluster at one end of the Spectrum in terms of science and technology, language, or physical or social isolation. However, their views regarding sex, gender, and sexuality may fall closer to the opposite end of the Spectrum. People of faith often have indicators that fall in different places along the Modernity Spectrum.

Some people of faith believe that one should not have sex until they are married. They believe sex should only happen inside marriage. Other people of faith, even within the same religion, may have a different view. They think sexuality is a personal choice. They believe love and commitment are more important than a "traditional" marriage. Some people of faith believe that a man can and should have multiple wives. Other people of faith within the same religion strongly believe the opposite.

Some people of faith strongly believe there are only two genders: male and female. They think these roles are given by God and should not change. They expect men and women to act in certain ways and do certain jobs. These beliefs affect family life, work, and how people live in their communities.

Other people of faith accept non-binary people and include LGBTQ+ people. They believe gender is more complex. They turn to science and scientific understandings to help shape their beliefs. They think faith should support everyone, no matter their gender identity.

Next

In the coming pages, we will look more closely at the Modernity Spectrum and how it affects religious life. We will look at real stories of cooperation and conflict. Through these stories, I hope to show that tolerance is not just an ideal—it is something we can build, one conversation at a time.

Chapter Two

Marker 1: "A" Truth versus "The" Truth

Living in today's world is often overwhelming. There are so many issues that demand our attention. News, social media, and constant updates make it feel like our heads might explode. People feel exhausted. Many just want to shut off their minds. They don't want to think. They want someone else to make decisions for them, to solve their problems, to tell them what to do.

Some people long for quick and easy answers. They want clear rules to follow, without doubt or confusion. Others want to step away completely. They withdraw from the world, hoping to escape the stress, fear, and uncertainty of modern life.

Uncertainty can be hard to handle. It can cause distress, sleepless nights, and even health problems. It can make people feel unsafe in their homes or afraid to step outside. In difficult times, people search for security. They look for something solid to hold onto. They want answers that never change.

This need for certainty leads some people to embrace strict beliefs. They want an absolute truth—one clear way to live life. They want to be told that there is only one right way to believe, act, and exist in the world. They crave rules that remove the burden of choice.

Non-modern practitioners of religion—both leaders and followers—often believe they have The Truth. They see their faith as the only correct way. The more non-modern the practice, the stronger the belief that this Truth is the only Truth. They insist that everyone must accept it—voluntarily or not. They see no room for different beliefs or perspectives.

For them, doubt is dangerous. Questioning is not allowed. Change is a threat. Their Truth must be defended at all costs, because to them, there is no other way.

But not everyone sees faith this way. Some believe in A Truth instead of The Truth. They accept that faith can be deeply personal. They understand that different people, different cultures, and different experiences can lead to different understandings of God, morality, and purpose. They find comfort in the idea that multiple truths can exist at the same time.

This chapter will explore these two ways of understanding faith—the belief in The Truth versus the belief in A Truth. We will look at how these beliefs shape the way people live, interact with others, and view the world around them. We will also ask an important question: Can people with different views of truth still find common ground?

The answers may surprise you.

Family: "A" Truth Versus "The" Truth

I grew up in a big, busy house. At one point, there were ten children living under our roof—my four brothers, my sister, four first cousins, and me. With so many kids, there was never a quiet moment.

But here's something I've realized over the years: even though we all grew up in the same house, with the same parents, our experiences of them were not the same. My mother is one person. My father is one person. Yet, when I sit with my siblings and cousins and we talk about them, I sometimes wonder—who are they talking about?

The way they describe my parents is often so different from my own experience. When we share stories, it sometimes feels like we are talking about completely different people. For each of my siblings and cousins their truth about my parents is 100% true for them, but it is not my truth. Sometimes, our memories match. Other times, they don't. I find myself thinking, *Surely they're not talking about MY mother! Surely they're not talking about MY father!*

We often laugh about this. How can we have grown up in the same house and see things so differently? And yet, we accept it. We know that each of us has our own truth based on our own experiences. No one demands that their version is the only right one. No one insists that we all remember things the exact same way. We can live together, knowing that each of us holds "A Truth" about our parents. But there is no single "The Truth."

When Families Demand "The" Truth

Not every family is like my own. In some families, different memories and experiences cause deep conflict. Instead of accepting that everyone has their own truth, they insist there is only one truth—The Truth. And if you do not accept The Truth, you are wrong.

In these families, disagreements over memories and experiences can lead to arguments, divisions, and even lasting resentment. The idea that multiple truths can exist is not allowed. There is only one version of events, one way to remember a parent, one way to tell a family story. To be part of the family, you must accept The Truth—even if it does not match your own experience.

Sometimes, these conflicts escalate. Family members take sides. They stop talking to each other. They refuse to invite certain relatives to weddings, holidays, or family gatherings. They spread rumors. They try to ruin reputations. In extreme cases, they even take each other to court over wills, property, or family businesses.

The same pattern exists in faith communities. Just like in families, some religious groups allow for different truths. They accept that people experience faith in different ways. Others demand that everyone believe in one Truth—their Truth. Those who disagree are seen as outsiders, traitors, or even enemies.

What Can We Learn from This?

If we can accept that our own siblings see our parents differently, why can't we accept that other people experience faith differently? If we can live in peace with family members who have different memories, why can't we do the same with people who have different beliefs?

This chapter explores faith communities navigating the struggle between A Truth and The Truth. It asks an important question: Is it possible to stay connected to people even when their truth is different from my own?

The answer, as we will see, can shape the way we live, the way we love, and the way we build relationships—with family, friends, and the world around us.

God/Higher Power/The Source/Creator: "A" Truth versus "The" Truth

As a rabbi and a chaplain, I often get asked a big question. People want to know how I can work with people of different faiths. They ask, "How can you help Christians, Muslims, Hindus, or people with no religion at all?" This is one of the most common questions which chaplains hear.

The answer is both simple and complex. My experience of God/Higher Power/The Source/Creator is true for me. But I also understand that others have different experiences. It is like how my siblings and cousins see my parents in different ways. We grew up in the same family, yet we may, and often do, remember things differently. Similarly, people connect to God in different ways. Their experience of faith is true for them, even if it is not my experience or my truth.

I do not need others to share my beliefs for my faith to be real. I can accept that their experience of God is different. I do not feel threatened by those differences.

Instead, I see them as a reflection of the vastness of the divine.

These different experiences have led to different religions, different sacred texts, and different ways of worshiping. I accept that my sacred texts and revelations are true for me. At the same time, others' own sacred texts and revelations are true for them. One does not cancel out the other.

This does not mean we must agree on everything. It also does not mean that all beliefs are exactly the same. But it does mean that we can respect each other's paths. Just as I would not tell someone that their memory of a family event is wrong, I do not tell others that their experience of faith is wrong.

This understanding allows chaplains like me to serve people of all faiths. It allows us to meet people where they are, without forcing our beliefs on them. It helps us support people in finding strength in their own faith, just as we find strength in ours.

Modernity: "A" Truth versus "The" Truth

"A" Truth versus "The" Truth is almost always a strong marker between those who practice a modern faith and those who practice their faith in non-modern ways. This is often one of the easiest determinations of where someone falls upon the Modernity Spectrum.

A Truth: Faith That Grows and Adapts

The more modern and integrated into the larger world of today, the more likely a person believes that their faith has "A Truth" for them but that there are also other "Truths" for other people. As uncomfortable as it might make them, and it often does, they accept that other people may follow different paths. They believe those paths can be just as true. They may not always agree, but they do not see different beliefs as a threat. Instead, they see them as part of a big and changing world. They are more willing to talk, listen, and learn from others. They try to find common ground with people of different faiths and beliefs.

One of the most important examples of someone who lived this belief is Pope Francis, head of the Roman Catholic Church. He stated in 2024 during a visit in Singapore: "If you start to fight: My religion is more important than yours, mine is true and yours isn't. Where will that lead us? There's only one God, and each of us has a language to arrive at God. Some are Sikh, Muslim, Hindu, Christian, and they are different paths [to God]."

People who believe in A Truth understand that religious teachings have changed over time. They see that faith must grow to stay relevant. They believe that religious leaders should interpret ancient texts in a way that makes sense today. They see history as proof that faith can evolve. They know that the world is not the same as it was thousands of years ago, and they accept that religion must change with it.

This does not mean that everything is open to change. They still hold core beliefs. They still follow traditions. But they allow for new ideas. They make room for science. They believe that God, or the divine, is big enough to handle questions. They believe that asking questions makes faith stronger, not weaker. They do not fear doubt. They embrace it as part of the journey.

These individuals often seek connection with people from different backgrounds. They are curious about other religions. They see faith as something that brings people together, not something that should separate them. They do not believe that one religion has all the answers. Instead, they believe that every faith tradition has wisdom to share.

For them, faith is not a set of rules that must be followed without question. It is a relationship. It is something that grows, changes, and deepens over time. They do not expect others to believe exactly as they do. They are comfortable with different beliefs existing side by side. They do not feel threatened when someone worships differently. They do not feel the need to prove that their way is the only way. They focus on kindness, justice, and making the world a better place.

People who hold A Truth often support education and critical thinking. They encourage their children to ask questions. They do not fear that learning about other beliefs will weaken their own. They teach that love, respect, and understanding are more important than strict rules. They believe that people should live their faith in a way that makes sense for them, while also respecting others.

The Truth: Faith That Must Be Defended

Faith practices that more strongly align with non-modern practices are more likely to present their tradition and their statements as "The Truth." This often is accompanied by an understanding that belief in anything else is wrong, corrupt, evil. That there is only one way to believe and to live life. Their way. End of story.

Those who hold The Truth see faith as unchanging. It was revealed once and must be followed exactly. They fear that change means corruption. They see questioning as rebellion. They do not seek dialogue. They seek obedience. To them, there is no need to learn from others. There is only the need to defend what they already know.

For these believers, faith is not a journey. It is a destination. There is no room for interpretation. Religious texts must be followed word for word, as they were written long ago. Traditions cannot be adjusted. What was true then must be true now and forever. Any deviation is dangerous.

This approach to faith often leads to strict rules. People must dress a certain way. They must pray in a specific manner. They must follow laws that were created in a very different time and place. There is no flexibility. There is no discussion. There is only The Truth, and it must be upheld at all costs.

People who hold The Truth often see the world in black and white. There is right, and there is wrong. There is no in-between. They believe their way is the only way. They see other beliefs as false, misguided, or even evil. They do not want to learn from other faiths. They do not want to listen to different ideas. They believe that allowing other views to exist weakens their own.

They also believe that those who do not follow The Truth are lost. They see it as their duty to bring others into their belief system. Some may do this through teaching and persuasion. Others may go further. Throughout history, people who hold The Truth have forced their beliefs on others. They have punished those who disagree. They have shut out those who question. They have created societies where only one way of thinking is allowed.

In some cases, those who hold The Truth may use fear to keep people in line. They warn of terrible consequences for those who stray. They teach that leaving the faith will result in suffering. They say that questioning is the same as betraying. In extreme cases, they may cut off family members or friends who do not follow the same path. They may refuse to associate with those who see the world differently.

Some groups that hold The Truth believe that the modern world is dangerous. They reject science, technology, and education. They isolate themselves to keep outside influences away. They may live in closed communities, refusing to interact with those who do not share their beliefs. Others remain in society but try to control the culture around them. They fight against change. They resist anything that challenges their way of life.

A Truth and The Truth: Two Different Worlds

The difference between A Truth and The Truth is at the heart of the Modernity Spectrum. It is a question of whether faith grows or stays the same. It is a question of whether people believe that others can hold different truths or if only one truth can exist. This is not just a religious question. It is a human question, one that shapes how we live, how we interact, and how we see the world.

People who believe in A Truth see faith as something that evolves. They welcome new ideas. Like Pope Francis, they accept that different people experience the divine in different ways. They focus on love, kindness, and learning from others.

People who believe in The Truth see faith as fixed. They fear that change will weaken their beliefs. They believe that questioning is dangerous. They see their way as the only way.

The way we answer this question determines whether we build bridges or walls. It determines whether we live in a world of understanding or a world of division. It determines whether we listen or whether we close our ears.

The choice is ours.

Chapter Three

Marker 2: Violence Regarding "The Other" and Purity Within

Introduction

I distinctly remember one of the conversations that led to my thinking about *A Truth versus The Truth* and the use of violence as a means of othering. A family member, after a terrorist attack on the Jewish community by someone of the Islamic faith, said: "Thank God we are nothing like them. We are a peace-loving people and would never do anything like this."

The first words out of my mouth were: "We are exactly like them."

I went on. There is no "them" and "us" when it comes to religious violence. All faiths have people who use violence. All faiths have people who use violence against those of other faiths. And at the same time, all faiths have people who use violence against those within their own faith. The violence in both cases often happens for the same reason — to "protect" a vision of what the extremist believes their faith should be.

When talking about this very sensitive subject, I have found it always best to start with the "I." This greatly helps to stop othering in a conversation. What does my faith tradition do? What examples come from within? By starting with what my religion does, I try to make it clear that I believe no religious group is better than any other when it comes to the use of violence. There is no Other.

I remember then mentioning to my family member the following examples of Jewish extremists using violence — both against non-Jews and also against Jews.

The first example I mentioned was the Cave of the Patriarchs massacre, which was carried out by Baruch Goldstein. The date — February 25, 1994 — coincided with the Jewish festival of Purim and also fell during the Muslim month of Ramadan. Goldstein murdered 29 Muslims in the attack, including six children aged fourteen or younger. Another 125 were wounded.

The Cave of the Patriarchs, or Tomb of the Patriarchs, is known to Jews by its biblical name, the Cave of Machpelah, and to Muslims as the Sanctuary of Abraham. It is a series of caves situated 19 miles south of Jerusalem, in the heart of the Old City of Hebron. According to the Abrahamic religions, the cave and the adjoining field were purchased by Abraham as a burial plot. The site is considered a holy place in Judaism, Christianity, and Islam.

Over the cave stands a large rectangular enclosure dating from the Herodian era. During Byzantine rule, a Christian basilica was built on the site. The structure was later converted into the Ibrahimi Mosque following the Muslim conquest of the region. After the Six-Day War of 1967, the mosque was divided, with half of it becoming a synagogue. Both Jews and Muslims were permitted to access their respective parts of the compound.

I indicated to my family member that it was my belief that it was not coincidental that Goldstein carried out the murders as Purim was being celebrated. To many ultra non-modern Jews, the festival of Purim is associated with a biblical reading that concerns Amalek, described in the Hebrew Bible as the enemy of the Israelites. In Jewish extremist non-modern rhetoric, Muslims are often identified as Amalek. In fact, on the eve of the massacre, Goldstein listened to a reading of the Scroll of Esther in the Hall of Abraham, found in the Tomb of the Patriarchs, and then spoke to others about the need to behave like Esther and save the Jewish people from destruction.

At 5:00 a.m. on February 25, around 800 Palestinian Muslims passed through the east gate of the cave to participate in Fajr, the first of the five daily Islamic prayers. Goldstein entered the mosque and opened fire with an assault rifle.

As I finished explaining this, my family member responded, "That was just one person." So I went on.

I reminded them of the practice, still common among ultra-Orthodox Jews in parts of Israel, of throwing rocks at other Jews to protest violations of religious law. For example, driving a car on the Sabbath is one such violation, and throwing stones in protest is practiced among ultra non-modern communities, such as the Hasidic community and the broader Haredi community.

I mentioned just one incident out of many. Throughout 2009, ultra non-modern Jews threw stones at passing cars in Jerusalem to protest Sabbath violations. Large-scale protests broke out in June and July of that year in response to the opening of a car park near the Old Quarter of Jerusalem. On August 9, Jerusalem city mayor Nir Barkat was stoned by dozens of Haredi demonstrators who blamed him for the car park's opening.

I then spoke about how many of these ultra non-modern Jews train their young members to pick up rocks and throw them — not at enemies of the Jewish people, but at other Jews.

Violence is not something that "others" do. It is something that happens within all faiths. It is often seen as a way to protect the "purity" of religious beliefs or communities. And it is not limited to any one group. It is a common behavior tied to where someone falls along the Modernity Spectrum.

Judaism is no exception.

Why Non-Modern Practitioners of Faith Use Violence

Violence isn't something that only "those people" do. Every religion has extremists — people who go too far trying to protect their version of The Truth. This happens when people are very focused on staying "pure" and can't accept others who are different.

While most religious people reject violence, some groups justify it as a way to defend their faith. They may believe that protecting their beliefs requires action, even if it harms others.

Non-modern groups often see themselves as guardians of an unchanging truth. Because of this, they may feel that any difference or disagreement is a threat—and threats must be fought, not welcomed.

Understanding how different traditions approach this issue helps us see where they fall on the Modernity Spectrum. Groups that reject violence in favor of dialogue and cooperation tend to be more modern. Those that rely on force or punishment to maintain religious purity tend to be more non-modern.

The use of violence is often about either "purity" within the faith or bullying and harassing those of other faiths. Some religious groups use violence to enforce religious laws or protect purity. Extremists in various traditions have attacked those who do not conform to their beliefs. They may see outsiders as a threat or view those who break religious rules as dangerous to the community. Violence can take many forms. It can be physical, such as attacks or punishments, or social, such as shunning and exclusion.

Here are examples of how non-modern religious violence has shown up in different parts of the world and in different religions:

- **India (Hindu Extremism):** In some parts of India, Hindu nationalist groups have attacked Muslims and Christians. One well-known example is the 2002 Gujarat riots, where Hindu mobs attacked Muslim neighborhoods. Hundreds were killed, and thousands were displaced. These acts were carried out by people who believed they were defending Hinduism from outside threats.
- **Africa (Christian Extremism in Uganda):** In Uganda, the *Lord's Resistance Army* (LRA), led by

Joseph Kony, has used violence to create a government based on a harsh interpretation of the Bible and the Ten Commandments. The group has forced children to become soldiers and uses religion to justify brutal attacks.

- **South America (Catholic Extremism in Colombia):** During the long civil conflict in Colombia, some Catholic paramilitary groups used religious language to justify their violence against Marxist rebels and those they saw as enemies of God. Though political reasons played a big role, religion was often used to give their actions a sense of divine approval.

- **Europe (Eastern Orthodox Extremism in the Balkans):** During the wars in the former Yugoslavia in the 1990s, some Serbian Orthodox Christians took part in violent campaigns against Muslims and Catholics. Religious identity was used to fuel hatred, and places of worship were destroyed in the name of defending faith and ethnic purity.

- **North America (Christian Extremism in the U.S.):** In the United States, some Christian extremist groups have attacked abortion clinics, claiming to act on behalf of God. The most infamous example is the bombing of a clinic in Alabama in 1998 and the murder of

Dr. George Tiller, a doctor who performed abortions, in 2009. These acts were carried out by people who believed violence was justified to stop what they saw as sin.

- **Islam (ISIS and the Islamic State):** In Iraq and Syria, the group known as ISIS has used violence to create what they called a "pure" Islamic state. They have attacked Muslims who did not follow their strict version of Islam, destroyed Christian and Kurdish-speaking Yazidi communities, and used brutal punishments in the name of religion. Most Muslims around the world strongly reject ISIS, but the group claims to be defending the faith.

- **Buddhism (Extremist Monks in Myanmar):** Although Buddhism is often associated with peace, some Buddhist monks in Myanmar have led violent movements against Muslims. The most well-known is the monk Ashin Wirathu, who encouraged attacks on the Rohingya Muslim minority. Entire villages were burned, and thousands of Rohingya fled the country. This was done in the name of protecting Buddhist identity.

- **Sikhism (Militant Sikh Separatism in India):** In the 1980s, some Sikh separatists in India fought to create a separate Sikh homeland called Khalistan. A few of these groups used violence against both Hindus and Sikhs who didn't support their cause. The situation led to a violent military action by the Indian government at the Golden Temple in Amritsar in 1984, which further escalated tensions. Some Sikh extremists believed they were fighting to preserve the purity of the Sikh faith and protect their identity.

But violence isn't always physical. It can also be quiet, invisible, and deeply personal. That's where we now turn—to social violence.

Social Violence: Exclusion as a Tool for Religious Purity

When Violence Isn't Physical

So far, I have looked at how some religious groups use physical violence to protect what they believe. I have shown how people in many different faiths have used attacks, threats, or punishment to fight for what they call "The Truth." These acts are harmful, and they often come from people who are very focused on keeping their group "pure."

But not all violence involves hurting someone's body. While physical violence is easier to see, emotional and social violence can be just as harmful—and sometimes more lasting. These types of harm often happen quietly but can deeply affect people's lives. It happens when people are left out, ignored, or pushed away by their family, friends, or religious community. This kind of harm is harder to see, but it can be just as painful.

Social violence often happens when someone questions a rule, chooses a different path, or doesn't fit in. For example, a person might be kicked out of their church or synagogue for loving someone of the same gender. A girl might be shamed for not wearing the "right" kind of religious clothing. Someone might stop believing everything their religion teaches — and suddenly, their whole community turns their back on them.

So why do people do this?

One reason is fear. Some religious communities believe that if they let in "new" ideas or accept people who are different, they will lose their special way of life. They worry their group will stop being "pure." To protect themselves, they cut off anyone who seems like a threat — even if that person is family.

This is where the Modernity Spectrum helps us understand what's going on.

At the non-modern end of the Modernity Spectrum are groups that try to hold tightly to old traditions and who don't want much contact with the modern world. They often believe there is only one truth, and that truth must be protected at all costs. If someone doesn't follow their exact way, they must be excluded or punished — not always with fists, but with silence, rejection, and shame.

At the modern end of the Modernity Spectrum are groups that also have strong beliefs but are open to change and conversation. They understand that people grow, change, ask questions, and may see the world differently. When someone in a modern community changes or challenges an idea, they are more likely to be listened to instead of pushed away.

In the next section, we will look at real stories of social violence from around the world. We'll see how people from different religions have used shunning, exclusion, and social pressure to control others. These are not just personal decisions — they are part of a bigger pattern. They show how religious communities, especially non-modern ones, use social violence to protect what they see as "purity" or "truth."

These examples are hard, but they are important. They remind us that real faith does not need fear to survive. And they help us ask a better question: how can we hold on to what we believe while still making space for others?

1. Amish Shunning (Meidung) – United States

In Amish communities, members who leave the church or violate core rules (like owning modern technology, marrying outside the faith, or refusing to repent) may be shunned, a practice known as *Meidung*. This means they are socially and even economically cut off — family members won't eat at the same table, do business with them, or engage in conversation. The goal is not only to punish the individual but to protect the spiritual purity and separation of the community. The act reinforces a boundary between "faithful" members and those considered to have brought in dangerous outside influences.

2. Jehovah's Witnesses Disfellowshipping – Global

Jehovah's Witnesses practice a formal process of *disfellowshipping* for members who commit what are seen as serious sins (such as celebrating birthdays, questioning church teachings, or forming relationships outside the group). Once disfellowshipped, the person is cut off socially, including by family members, unless they repent. This practice is used to keep the community "clean" from spiritual contamination and to discourage others from disobedience. Those who leave often report deep trauma from the sudden isolation — not just from friends but from parents, children, or siblings.

3. Muslim Women and Hijab Enforcement – Middle East and Diaspora Communities

In some conservative Muslim societies — including parts of Iran, Afghanistan, and even within diaspora communities — women who choose to remove the hijab (headscarf) or wear more modern clothing can face public shaming, exclusion, or harassment. Families may limit their participation in community life, or neighbors may gossip or threaten them. These acts are justified as protecting the "honor" of the family or the religious purity of Islamic modesty laws, even though many Muslims worldwide support a woman's right to choose. The social pressure enforces conformity and deters others from questioning tradition.

4. LGBTQ+ Exclusion in Conservative Christian Families – United States and Beyond

In many fundamentalist or evangelical Christian homes, coming out as LGBTQ+ can lead to being disowned, sent to conversion therapy, or forced out of the home. Some are completely excluded from family gatherings or church life. This exclusion is often framed as "tough love" or "protecting biblical truth," especially verses cited against same-sex relationships. The underlying fear is that embracing LGBTQ+ identities might "contaminate" the moral clarity or purity of the family or church.

5. Religious Conversion and Social Ostracism – India

In some Hindu-majority villages in India, when someone converts to Christianity or Islam, they may face community-level ostracism, including being barred from drawing water, denied entry to markets, or excluded from social ceremonies like weddings. In some cases, entire families are boycotted. These acts are often driven by Hindu nationalist ideas that view religious conversion as a threat to the cultural and spiritual purity of the village or nation. Local councils may even pressure converts to "reconvert" through shaming or economic punishment.

6. Ex-Ultra-Orthodox Jews and Family Exclusion – Israel, U.S., and Europe

Those who leave Haredi (Ultra-Orthodox) Jewish communities — often called *off the derech* ("off the path") — may experience total disconnection from parents, siblings, and friends. They are often no longer invited to family events or are spoken about in hushed tones. Some are treated as though they are spiritually dead. This practice serves as a warning to others: questioning strict religious life is not just discouraged, it threatens the identity and purity of the entire group. In many cases, community leaders frame the departure as a kind of infection that must be isolated to protect the rest.

Summary: Violence, Truth, and the Modernity Spectrum

This chapter was about how some religious people use violence to protect what they believe is true. It showed that violence is not just something done by "other" people. It can happen in any religion, anywhere in the world. The chapter also explained that violence can happen not just to people from other religions, but also to people from the same religion who don't follow the rules exactly.

The big idea is this: violence is often used to protect purity. Some people believe that their religion must stay pure and never change. They think that anyone who brings in new ideas, different behaviors, or questions might "pollute" the faith. So they fight back. Sometimes with words, sometimes with actions, and sometimes with force.

To help us understand this, we use the Modernity Spectrum to gauge how religious people relate to the modern world.

At one end are non-modern groups. These groups try to keep things exactly the way they've always been. They follow old traditions very strictly. They may fear the outside world. They may not want to change or listen to new ideas. They often believe that their way is the only right way. And they may feel they must protect the truth — even with force if necessary.

At the other end are modern groups. These people also care deeply about their religion. But they believe that faith can grow. They are more open to change, conversation, and learning. They don't think everyone has to believe exactly the same. They try to live in peace with people who are different.

This chapter showed that violence is often tied to where a person or group falls on the Modernity Spectrum. Non-modern groups are more likely to feel threatened by change. When they feel scared, they may try to control others. They may use fear, punishment, or even violence to keep their beliefs safe. But this kind of safety is built on fear, not strength.

Modern groups are more likely to deal with change through discussion and understanding. They may still have strong beliefs, but they do not try to force others to agree. They know that the world is full of different people, and that faith does not have to mean fighting.

The chapter also explained that violence is not just about anger. It is often about power and control. When people feel their group is in danger, they may use violence to protect it. But that doesn't make it right. Just because something is done in the name of religion does not mean it is good or holy.

In the end, this chapter reminds us that real faith does not need to hurt others. Real strength in religion comes from love, not fear. The Modernity Spectrum helps us see this clearly. It teaches us to look not just at what people believe, but how they live with others who believe differently.

Chapter Four

Marker 3: Physical and Social Isolation

A Visit to Isolated Non-Modern Communities

When I visited Mea Shearim in Jerusalem, it felt like I had stepped into the past. This Jewish neighborhood follows very strict rules. Signs told visitors to dress modestly. Outsiders were not welcome.

On the Sabbath, no cars are allowed. Strangers are treated with caution. If you do not follow their rules, you may be yelled at or asked to leave.

People here live differently from most of modern society. They wear old-style clothing. They speak Yiddish, not Hebrew. Their daily life is separate from the modern world.

I saw something similar in Amish Country in Pennsylvania. The Amish also live without many modern tools. They farm and make things by hand. They speak Pennsylvania Dutch, not English. They live simply and apart from others.

Both the Jews of Mea Shearim and the Amish have chosen to live outside the modern world. They believe this protects their way of life. But it also means they lose access to things like new knowledge and technology.

Introduction: Isolation and the Modernity Spectrum

Many religious groups choose to live apart from the modern world. Some build towns or neighborhoods that keep outsiders away.

They limit contact with modern society. They may ban the internet, control what their kids learn, or avoid people who are not part of their group. They believe this protects their values.

Other religious groups do the opposite. They live in modern society and mix their faith with modern ideas.

How much a group isolates itself shows where it falls on the Modernity Spectrum.

Ways Non-Modern Faith Communities May Physically Isolate

Some groups live in places far away from others. Others build their own towns. These groups want to stay separate.

Here are some examples:

- The Bruderhof live in farming villages and avoid modern jobs.

- Kiryas Joel and New Square in New York are Hasidic Jewish towns with strict rules.

- The Harari in Ethiopia stay separate from nearby modern groups.

- Aghori Sadhus in India live in hidden places and follow very old customs.

- Jain monks in India live alone and avoid all modern things.

- Hutterites in the U.S. and Canada live in shared farms.

- Mennonite groups in South America live in farming towns without modern amenities and conveniences.

All of these groups avoid modern life in different ways. But they all believe physical separation protects their traditions.

Extreme Cases of Isolation and Its Consequences

Some groups take isolation too far. This can cause real harm.

- Jonestown: In 1978, over 900 people followed Jim Jones to a jungle in Guyana. They could not leave. One day, they were forced to drink poison.

They died because they had no way out.

- Aum Shinrikyo: This cult in Japan lived in closed camps. People were brainwashed. In 1995, they used poison gas in the Tokyo subway. Thirteen people died.

- Ural Pagans: In Russia, this group lived in caves. They never came out. Some went blind from the darkness. Others became sick or died.

Extreme isolation can destroy lives. It may begin with a wish to stay pure. But it can end in suffering.

Final Thoughts: Physical Isolation on the Modernity Spectrum

Some groups avoid modern life but still talk to the outside world. Others cut off all contact.

This chapter reminds us that how and why faith groups choose to isolate is deeply tied to where they fall on the Modernity Spectrum.

The Amish may avoid cars and electricity but still sell things to outsiders. Hasidic Jews may live in their own towns but still use doctors and phones.

Other groups go much further. They allow no contact. This can become dangerous. People may suffer or even die.

Isolation can protect faith. But it can also lead to pain.

The Modernity Spectrum helps us see the choices these groups make. Some keep a balance. Others move far from modern life and risk harm.

Ways Non-Modern Faith Communities May Socially Isolate

Some groups don't live far away but still keep their lives separate. This is social isolation.

They do it in different ways:

Marriage Restrictions

Many groups say you must marry within the faith. Marrying outside is not allowed. If you break the rule, you may be punished or cast out.

Examples:

- Druze in the Middle East: Marrying outsiders means being cut off.

- Jehovah's Witnesses: Marrying outside may lead to being ignored by family.

- Yazidis: Those who marry non-Yazidis are forced to leave the community.

- Ultra-Orthodox Jews: People may be shunned or have funerals held for them if they marry outsiders.

- Amish: Marrying outside the group often means being shunned.

Work and Economic Separation

Some groups do not work for big companies. They make their own jobs and sell only to each other.

Examples:

- Amish: Work on farms or small shops. Avoid technology.

- Hutterites: Share work and income. Live simply.

- Mennonites in South America: Live in closed farming towns.

This makes it hard for people to leave. If they do, they lose their job and support.

Medical and Healthcare Isolation

Some groups avoid doctors and medicine. They believe only faith can heal.

Examples:

- Christian Scientist: Use prayer, not medicine.

- Amish: Often avoid vaccines and hospitals.

- Faith healing churches: Trust only prayer to cure illness.

This can lead to death from treatable sickness.

Political and Civic Disengagement

Some groups do not vote or serve in government. They believe they should only follow God.

Examples:
- Jehovah's Witnesses: Do not vote or salute flags.
- Amish: Do not join politics.
- Hutterites: Avoid all government systems.
- Quakers: Some avoid the military and politics.
- Bruderhof: Stay out of politics.

They do this to keep their faith pure. But it also means they cannot help shape laws that affect them.

Final Thoughts: Social Isolation on the Modernity Spectrum

Groups isolate in many ways. Some only marry within the group. Others avoid modern jobs, doctors, or politics.

Isolation can keep faith strong. But it can also take away freedom and safety.

Each group must choose how much to allow in and how much to keep out. The Modernity Spectrum shows us where those choices fall.

In later chapters, we will look more closely at isolation through language, education, technology, and dress. Each shows us how people of faith balance old ways with the modern world.

Chapter Five

Marker 4: Modesty: Dress, Clothing, and Physical Contact

I grew up in the Deep South in the 1960s and 1970s. I have a degree in Agriculture from a Southern land-grant university. Without knowing it, I learned that how some women dressed showed what they believed and where they might fall on the Modernity Spectrum. In particular, I saw that many women who followed non-modern forms of Christianity dressed a certain way.

They always wore dresses. The dresses were below the knee, and they wore hose or stockings to cover any part of their legs the dress did not cover. Their dresses often had sleeves below the elbow, even during the hot summer. The neckline was high and often went up to the neck.

I moved to New York City in 1991. After a while, I noticed that many women in New York dressed the same way. I thought they were non-modern Christians. But from everything I had read, there were very few non-modern Christians in the city. My eyes were telling me something different.

One day, I saw a family of ultra non-modern Jews, including the father who was dressed in a black suit that looked like it came from another era. Suddenly, it dawned on me. The women I had thought were non-modern Christians were actually non-modern Jews. I was stunned. They dressed almost exactly the same! That day, I learned how modesty and religious beliefs shape how people dress. It's a lesson I have never forgotten.

Over time, I realized that if a non-modern Christian, a Jewish, and a Muslim woman were in the same room, and you didn't know their religions, you might not be able to tell them apart. They all dress alike. Long dresses. Long sleeves. Legs always covered. Head coverings in one form or another.

Introduction

Othering often happens around dress and clothing. I have often heard people say things like, "Look at that woman wearing that head covering. So typical of X religion. Why can't they just fit in? People in my religion would never dress like that." Or, "Look at that man. Why does he dress that way? He clearly doesn't want to be American. Thank God no one in my religion looks like that."

People often forget that every religion has people who dress a certain way because of their beliefs about modesty. Many religions have modesty rules, especially for women. People often forget that many religions have modesty rules not just for women, but for men too. In some non-modern communities, men dress in very specific ways to show their faith and values. If you put a Hasidic Jewish man from Brooklyn, a Salafi Muslim man from Cairo, an Old Order Mennonite farmer from Pennsylvania, and a Hindu priest from a rural village in India all in the same room, you might be surprised by how similar they look. They might all wear long beards, loose-fitting clothes, and head coverings. Even though they follow different religions, their clothing shows a shared desire to separate from modern styles and stay close to tradition.

Modesty rules often reflect a group's ideas about morality and purity. Some communities believe that covering the body shows respect for God and tradition. Others see modest dress as a way to separate from the outside world. Some religions do not focus much on dress at all. They believe faith is shown through actions, not clothing.

Modesty and Faith

Modesty is a concern in almost all faith traditions because it reflects deeper values about respect, humility, and self-control. Most religions teach that how we present ourselves—through clothing, behavior, or speech—should reflect the dignity of the individual and the sacredness of life.

Here are some key reasons I have heard about why modesty matters in many religions.

1. Modesty shows respect for oneself and others.

In many traditions, modesty is seen as a way to honor your own body and to avoid making others uncomfortable. It's about not drawing too much attention to yourself in a way that might distract from spiritual or community life.

2. Modesty reflects humility.

Faith often calls people to be humble—not boastful or proud. Modest dress and speech help remind people that spiritual worth is more important than physical appearance or status.

3. Modesty supports community values.

Some religions believe that when people dress or act modestly, it creates a safer, more respectful community. It helps set clear boundaries and shared expectations.

4. Modesty connects the body to spiritual goals.

In traditions like Islam, Judaism, Christianity, Hinduism, and Buddhism, modesty is often linked to ideas of purity or self-discipline. Covering the body or speaking carefully is not about shame, but about focusing the heart and mind on God.

5. Modesty can be a way of resisting modern values.

For more non-modern faith groups, modesty becomes a way to stand apart from a world they see as too focused on fashion, fame, or sexuality. It marks identity and holds onto tradition.

In short, modesty is not just about clothing nor behavior nor speech—it's about character. It reflects how a person lives their values every day. And that's why it continues to be so important in religious life across the globe.

Modesty and Faith on the Modernity Spectrum

Modesty is important in almost every religion. It is about how people dress, how they speak, and how they act. Most faiths teach that we should be respectful, humble, and careful about how we present ourselves. Modesty is one way people show these values.

But how people practice modesty can look very different—and where a group falls on the Modernity Spectrum helps explain why.

Modern Faith Communities and Modesty

Modern religious groups often teach modesty as a value, but they allow people to make their own choices.

They believe modesty should come from the heart, not just from rules. People may choose respectful clothing but still dress in ways that fit modern life. Most modern groups also allow casual touch and eye contact between men and women. Shaking hands or making friendly eye contact is usually seen as polite, not immodest.

- In many modern Christian churches in the U.S. or Europe, women may wear dresses or pants, and men may wear jeans or suits. This applies both during worship services and at community events. There are usually no strict dress rules—just a general expectation to dress respectfully.

- In modern Muslim communities in places like Indonesia or Malaysia, some women wear the hijab (headscarf), while others do not. Both choices are accepted.

- In modern Jewish communities like Reform or Conservative synagogues in the U.S., women may choose to wear short sleeves or trousers, and men may or may not wear a yarmulke (skullcap). There is freedom to decide.

- In modern Hindu families in big cities like Mumbai or London, women may wear saris or jeans, depending on the situation. The focus is on modesty in spirit, not following a strict code.

In these examples, modesty is still important, but it works alongside modern culture and personal choice. These groups are on the modern side of the Modernity Spectrum.

Non-Modern Faith Communities and Modesty

Non-modern religious groups often have strict rules about modesty. These rules may be based on old traditions or sacred texts. People in these groups believe that following modesty rules shows obedience to God and helps protect the community from outside influence.

In many of these communities, men and women do not touch people of the opposite sex unless they are close family. Some also teach that people should avoid looking directly at someone of the opposite sex for more than a brief moment.

Below are some examples of how modesty is practiced in some non-modern faith communities.

- In ultra-Orthodox Jewish communities in Israel or Brooklyn, women often wear long skirts, long sleeves, and cover their hair with wigs or scarves. Men wear black suits, white shirts, and hats, even in hot weather. They avoid touch and often limit eye contact between men and women.

- In conservative Muslim communities in Afghanistan, Iran, or parts of Pakistan, women must wear a hijab (headscarf) or even a burqa, which covers the entire body. Men may be expected to grow beards and dress modestly. Touch between unrelated men and women is usually forbidden.

- In some traditional Christian groups like the Amish or Hutterites in the U.S. and Canada, both men and women dress in plain clothes. Women wear bonnets and long dresses. Men wear dark pants and suspenders. Gender separation is common, and physical contact is limited.

- In non-modern Hindu villages in parts of India, women may not be allowed to show their hair or legs in public. Wearing traditional dress like a sari or salwar kameez is expected at all times.

- In some Buddhist communities in Thailand or Sri Lanka, monks and nuns shave their heads and wear simple robes. Laypeople also dress modestly when entering a temple—no shorts or tight clothing—and men and women do not touch monks or nuns.

In these examples, modesty is used as a way to separate from modern values. It sends a clear message that the group wants to stay close to its religious roots. These groups are on the non-modern side of the Modernity Spectrum.

How Modesty Shows Us the Where a Group/Person Should be Placed on the Modernity Spectrum

The Modernity Spectrum helps us see how different faith groups approach modesty. Some see it as a flexible value.

Others treat it as a strict rule. Some leave the choice up to the person. Others expect everyone to follow the same standards.

To understand where a faith group and those who practice it fall on the Modernity Spectrum, ask questions like:

- Who sets the rules for modesty—individuals or leaders?

- Are people free to choose, or are there punishments for not following the dress code?

- Does the group try to blend into the modern world, or stand apart from it?

So even though almost all religions care about modesty, how they show it—and why—can be very different. That's what the Modernity Spectrum helps us understand.

Chapter Six

Marker 5: Science and Technology

Introduction

I remember the first time I visited Amish Country in Pennsylvania. It felt like stepping into a different world. Horse-drawn buggies were everywhere! I was surprised to see special parking spots for buggies in front of large stores. As I drove through the countryside, I noticed that many homes and farms had no electricity lines. I learned that most Amish homes do not have phones inside. Instead of tractors, I saw farmers using horses to plow fields.

I also realized their clothing was different. All of it was sewn by hand. When I looked closely, I noticed something unusual—there were no zippers on their clothes. Some outfits did not even have buttons. Instead, they used hooks and eyes to fasten their garments. Every detail of their lifestyle showed a deep commitment to rejecting modern technology.

I have had similar experiences in Hasidic Jewish neighborhoods, both in the United States and Israel. Walking through these communities, I noticed how quiet they were. When windows were open, I never heard radios or televisions. Many homes do not have computers, and internet use is closely restricted. Smartphones are discouraged. Instead, some Hasidic Jews use "kosher phones"—basic flip phones with no internet, social media, or texting. While some own cars, many rely on community-organized transportation rather than driving vehicles with modern technology.

As a hospital chaplain, I have also learned about Christian Scientists. Many of them refuse medical treatments such as surgeries, vaccines, and medications. Instead, they rely on Christian Science practitioners for spiritual healing. In extreme cases, this has led to legal battles, especially when children have died from preventable illnesses.

Most Faith Practitioners Accept Modern Science and Technology

While some religious groups reject certain aspects of modernity, most faith communities around the world embrace science and technology. They see no conflict between faith and progress. Many religious leaders encourage education and scientific discovery, believing that knowledge can improve society. Some even argue that science and religion work together to help people understand both the physical and spiritual world.

Below are examples of religious leaders who have studied science and incorporated it into their beliefs.

Pope Francis

Pope Francis, the recent head of the Roman Catholic Church, was a leading example of a faith leader who valued science. Before becoming a priest, he studied at a technical school in Buenos Aires, Argentina. He earned a diploma as a chemical technician and worked in a food laboratory, analyzing food quality and safety.

His scientific background has influenced his approach to issues like climate change, environmental responsibility, and the relationship between faith and science. In 2015, he wrote *Laudato Si'*, an encyclical that emphasized the importance of science in solving environmental problems. He often spoke about how reason, scientific research, and ethics must work together in medicine and technology.

Mehdi Golshani

Mehdi Golshani is a Muslim physicist from Iran. He is known for his work in particle physics, quantum mechanics, and the philosophy of science. He earned his Ph.D. in physics and became a professor at Sharif University of Technology. He also served as the director of the Institute of Humanities and Cultural Studies in Tehran.

Golshani has worked to promote scientific study in the Muslim world. He believes that science and faith do not have to be in conflict. Instead, he argues that religion can inspire curiosity about the universe. He has written books and given lectures on how Islamic teachings and scientific discoveries can complement each other.

Willem B. Drees

Willem B. Drees is a Dutch scholar who has contributed to discussions on science and religion. He holds two Ph.D. degrees—one in theoretical physics and another in theology. He has been a professor of philosophy of religion at Leiden University and Tilburg University.

Drees studies religious naturalism, a way of understanding religion without relying on supernatural beliefs. He writes about how scientific knowledge can help explain the world while still leaving room for spiritual meaning. His work encourages dialogue between scientists and religious thinkers.

Aga Khan IV (Karim Al-Hussaini)

Aga Khan IV, also known as Prince Karim Al-Husseini Aga Khan, was the 49th Imam of the Nizari Ismailis, a branch of Shia Islam. He studied at Harvard University, where he began with engineering before switching to Islamic history.

As a spiritual leader, he emphasized education and development. He founded the Aga Khan Development Network, which focuses on health, education, and culture, particularly in Africa and Asia. He believed that scientific knowledge and faith should work together to improve people's lives. His projects have helped bring modern medicine, education, and technology to underserved communities.

Bhaktisvarupa Damodara Swami

Bhaktisvarupa Damodara Swami, born Thoudam Damodara Singh in 1937 in Toubul, Manipur, India, was a leader in the International Society for Krishna Consciousness (ISKCON). He earned a Ph.D. in physical organic chemistry from the University of California, Irvine, in 1974.

As the international director of the Bhaktivedanta Institute, he worked to connect science and spirituality. He organized conferences, wrote books, and encouraged dialogue between scientists and religious scholars. He believed that studying the natural world could deepen spiritual understanding.

Review

While some religious groups limit their use of modern technology, many faith leaders have embraced science. They see education, medicine, and technology as tools that can improve lives while still honoring spiritual values. From Pope Francis to Mehdi Golshani, religious leaders around the world have shown that faith and science do not have to be in opposition. Instead, they can work together to create a better future.

Groups and Countries that Reject Modern Science and Technology

While many religious groups accept science and technology, some reject them for religious reasons. These groups believe modern technological advancements conflict with their faith. Some avoid electricity, cars, and the internet. Others reject modern medicine, choosing prayer or traditional healing instead. Below are examples of groups and countries that limit science and technology due to religious beliefs.

It is important to note that while some religious groups reject parts of modern healthcare, science, and technology, they accept other aspects of modern life and technology. Those in this group are often indistinguishable from most of their neighbors.

Hasidic Jewish Communities (United States, Israel, Europe)

As noted in the introduction to this chapter, some Hasidic Jewish communities strictly control technology. Many families do not have televisions or internet access. If they use phones, they prefer "kosher phones" that block internet and social media. Some avoid computers and keep their children away from modern entertainment.

As a health care chaplain, I have learned first-hand that medical science is also a sensitive issue. In many cases, community rabbis decide what medical treatments are acceptable. Today, some Hasidic groups even refuse vaccines or certain medical treatments.

The Amish (United States, Canada)

As I wrote about in the introduction of this chapter, the Amish are a Christian group that rejects most modern technology. They believe in a simple way of life. It is often easy to spot Amish communities. They do not use electricity in their homes, and thus, there are no power lines going to their houses. They travel by horse and buggy instead of cars. Their clothing is handmade, and they do not use zippers or buttons. Some Amish allow battery-powered tools, but others do not.

The Amish also limit their use of modern medicine. They prefer natural remedies and faith healing. Many do not get vaccinated, and some avoid hospitals. Instead of going to doctors, they may seek help from community healers. Their rejection of modern science comes from their belief in living separately from the outside world.

The Hutterites (United States, Canada)

The Hutterites are a Christian group similar to the Amish, but they live in large colonies. They avoid many modern conveniences. Most Hutterites do not have personal cars, televisions, or internet. Their homes and communities are simple and separate from modern society.

Hutterites also have strict views on medical science. While they accept some modern healthcare, they prefer natural remedies. Some Hutterite communities do not vaccinate their children. They believe that too much contact with doctors and hospitals goes against their religious way of life. Their goal is to remain separate and faithful to their traditions.

Taliban-Controlled Areas (Afghanistan)

The Taliban enforces strict religious laws in Afghanistan. They limit scientific education, especially for women and girls. Many schools do not teach modern science or technology. Instead, religious studies are the main focus. Some subjects, like biology and evolution, are removed from textbooks.

Medical advancements are also restricted. Women in Taliban-controlled areas often struggle to get medical care. Many hospitals have strict rules, and female doctors are rare. The Taliban believes that modern science should not replace religious teachings. Because of this,

Afghanistan faces challenges in healthcare, education, and technology.

Christian Science (Global, U.S.)

Christian Science is a religious movement that teaches faith healing. Christian Science members generally use technology in everyday life. They drive cars, use electricity, have phones, and use the internet like most people. They do not reject modern conveniences or scientific advancements in fields like engineering or communication.

However, followers believe that prayer, not medicine, is the best way to heal sickness. Many reject modern medical treatments, including surgeries, vaccines, and prescription drugs. Instead, they turn to Christian Science practitioners for spiritual healing.

This belief has caused controversy, especially when children have died from preventable illnesses. Some parents have been taken to court for refusing medical care for their children. While Christian Scientists can choose medical treatment, many rely only on prayer. They believe that sickness is not real, but rather a challenge of faith.

The Laestadian Lutherans (Finland, Sweden, Norway, Russia, United States)

Laestadian Lutherans (found mainly in Finland, Sweden, Norway, Russia, and the United States) do use technology in general. They drive cars, use electricity, have smartphones, and use the internet. They are not like the Amish or other groups that completely reject modern technology.

However, they tend to live simply and discourage excessive use of technology, especially when it might lead to worldly distractions or moral concerns. For example:

• Television and social media are often discouraged or avoided because they can bring unwanted secular influences.

• Modest living is encouraged, so flashy or luxury items might be frowned upon.

• Traditional values are emphasized, so technology is often used in practical ways rather than for entertainment or social trends.

Despite their conservative views, Laestadian Lutherans do not reject modern science or medicine. They go to doctors, use hospitals, and accept medical treatments, including vaccines.

In summary, Laestadians use technology in general but with a focus on simplicity, practicality, and avoiding moral dangers.

Conclusion: The Spectrum of Science and Technology in Religious Communities

Religious groups vary widely in how they approach science and technology. As noted in the first section of this chapter, some fully embrace modern advancements. As shown in the second section, others reject certain aspects of science, technology, and medicine for religious or cultural reasons. The groups discussed in this chapter illustrate the breadth of difference in this aspect of the Modernity Spectrum: some limit their use of modern tools and medicine, while others live fully within modern society but maintain restrictions in specific areas.

At one end of the Modernity Spectrum, groups like the Amish and Hutterites reject most modern technology, choosing a simple, agrarian lifestyle. Their rejection of electricity, cars, and modern medicine is based on a desire to remain separate from the outside world. Hasidic Jewish communities take a different approach, limiting access to the internet, social media, and secular education while still using some modern conveniences. Christian Science followers, in contrast, generally use technology in everyday life but reject modern medical treatments, relying on prayer for healing.

Meanwhile, the Taliban in Afghanistan enforces religious restrictions that severely limit scientific education and medical advancements, especially for women. This is an example of how a government can impose religious beliefs to control access to modern knowledge. It shows one set of practices at the very edge of the non-modern end of the Modernity Spectrum. At the other end, Laestadian Lutherans use technology but encourage simplicity and avoid excessive worldly distractions.

These examples show that religious beliefs can influence how people interact with modern science and technology in many ways. While some reject all modern advancements, others selectively limit their use based on moral or spiritual concerns. Most religious groups today, however, fully accept science and technology as a part of life and seek to balance faith with progress.

Chapter Seven

Marker 6: Education

Introduction

Some religious groups encourage learning, science, and philosophy. They believe that knowledge strengthens faith. They see education as a way to explore the world and better understand religious teachings. Many religious schools teach a wide range of subjects, from history and literature to math and science. Some faith traditions even encourage higher education and academic study.

Other groups fear that secular education will weaken faith. They limit what their children can learn, restricting subjects like evolution, philosophy, or history. They may only allow religious texts to be studied. Some communities discourage higher education altogether, believing it leads people away from their faith. The way a religious group approaches education can tell us a lot about where they fall on the Modernity Spectrum.

One Family – Two Thoughts on Education

My aunt is deeply worried about the future of her grandchildren. She has a doctorate in nursing. She was the dean of a major nursing program. She volunteers at the Metropolitan Museum of Art. Despite her own accomplishments, she is uncertain about how her grandchildren will manage in the modern world. She fears they may not be equipped to earn a living or navigate life beyond the narrow insular community in which they were raised. Even if they want to leave, she wonders whether they have the education and skills to thrive outside of it.

Her grandchildren were born into and raised in a very non-modern Jewish family. Her daughter and her husband joined their non-modern faith community as adults. The daughter has a law degree from Harvard.

The husband is equally educated. Each was educated in mixed-sex schools. Both parents have advanced secular educational training. And both were in agreement that they wanted their children educated differently than they were.

Their children were educated in private, faith-based, non-modern religious schools. Boys in one set of schools. Girls in another. The boys had hours of daily study in religious subjects. Very little of their education was in English, even though they live in an English-speaking world. They were not taught English, math, science, history, civics, or many other subjects required in secular schools.

One report on the school system they attend accurately describes a major reason why the parents sent their children to these private religious schools:

"The twin evils of Nazi Germany and the Soviet Union targeted Jews' very existence and their ability to openly practice their religion, respectively. Thus, the primacy of preserving their culture and religion is at the heart of their schools."

On the other hand, New York State has repeatedly found that the school systems the children attended do not meet basic educational standards. In July of 2023, The State found that, "Eighteen private Jewish schools run by New York City's politically powerful Hasidic community deprived thousands of students the required secular education in English, math, science and social studies that they need to function successfully outside their religious enclaves, according to findings from an eight-year investigation by New York City school officials."

For my aunt, this is the heart of her concern. She respects her daughter's faith and the community her family has chosen, but she worries that love and devotion aren't enough to prepare a child for the world beyond that community. With my aunt's background in education and healthcare, she has spent her life believing that knowledge empowers people to make choices. She fears that without a strong education including secular subjects, her grandchildren may not have real choices at all. To her, the issue isn't just about academics—it's about whether they will have the tools to survive, adapt, and flourish if life ever pulls them beyond the boundaries of the world they were raised in.

Education in Faith Communities

Religious and secular education taking place in religious schools is found in many places throughout the world. Here are just a few types:

- Roman Catholic Parochial School Systems – Roman Catholic schools around the world are often run by religious orders and parishes, offering both secular curriculum and instruction in Catholic doctrine, sacraments, and values. Many are affiliated with the country's national Catholic Bishops' Conference.

- Buddhist Temple-based Monastic Schools – Many young Thai boys attend Wat schools (temple schools) where they receive education from Buddhist monks. These schools emphasize Buddhist teachings, meditation, and morality alongside basic secular subjects.

- Anglican Schools – Australia has a well-established system of Anglican schools that integrate Christian education, chapel services, and moral development alongside academic studies. These schools may serve both religious and secular students.

- Hindu Faith Schools – The UK has state-funded Hindu schools such as Krishna Avanti Primary School, which combine the national curriculum with teachings from Hindu scriptures, Sanskrit, yoga, and emphasis on values like dharma and ahimsa.

- Islamic Madrasas (also spelled madrassas) Schools – Madrasas are Islamic religious schools found throughout the Muslim world. They provide instruction primarily in the Qur'an, Hadith (Prophetic traditions), Islamic jurisprudence (Fiqh), theology (Aqidah), and Arabic grammar. While many madrasas focus exclusively on religious education, some also incorporate limited secular subjects. Instruction typically takes place in dedicated religious schools, though some are affiliated with mosques.

Religious schools are not found everywhere in the world. Some countries, like France, China, the Netherlands, and North Korea, limit or ban them. These governments want schools to teach the same ideas to everyone. They worry that religious schools might teach things that go against what the government believes or wants.

Where Schools Fall on the Modernity Spectrum and Why

A general rule is this: the more a school teaches about the wider world, the more modern it is. The more a school limits learning to only religious ideas, the more non-modern it is. To figure out where a school falls on the Modernity Spectrum, you can ask some simple questions:

- What subjects are taught?

- Are students allowed to ask questions?

- Are they taught to think for themselves?

- Are they prepared to live and work in the modern world?

A modern religious school teaches both faith and modern subjects. This includes science, math, technology, history, and literature. It allows students to explore different ideas and ask hard questions. These schools often prepare students for college, careers, and life in many cultures.

A non-modern religious school avoids most secular subjects. It teaches mainly religious texts, rules, and customs. It may not teach modern science, world history, or other religions. These schools want to protect their students from outside ideas.

Some religious schools do not teach modern subjects at all. They focus only on their sacred texts, rules, and traditions. These schools are called non-modern because they avoid new ideas, science, or other cultures. Their goal is to protect their faith, not to prepare students for the modern world.

Some Christian communities in the United States run non-modern schools. These schools may teach that the world is only a few thousand years old. They reject evolution and teach that God created everything in six days. Their goal is to keep children inside a Bible-based worldview.

In Israel, many Haredi Jewish schools are extremely non-modern and do not teach math, English, or science. Boys are taught religious texts full-time from a young age. These schools prepare students to stay in their religious world. They do not prepare them to work in jobs outside of it.

In Afghanistan, many madrasas focus almost only on the Qur'an and Islamic law. Students often memorize verses instead of learning how to ask questions or solve problems. These schools do not usually teach science or world history. They aim to raise faithful Muslims, not modern citizens.

In parts of rural India, some Hindu religious schools teach only basic reading and religious stories. They do not teach subjects like chemistry or geography. Parents send their children to these schools to protect them from outside beliefs. They worry that modern schools will weaken their culture or values.

In Saudi Arabia, some Islamic schools only teach religion. Students learn Islamic rules, prayers, and how to live as good Muslims. There is little room for science, foreign languages, or modern history. These schools try to build strong faith, not modern knowledge.

Non-modern schools often believe the outside world is dangerous to their way of life. They want to raise children who will follow their religious path completely. They fear that modern learning will lead to doubt, rebellion, or loss of faith. That is why these schools stay far from the modern end of the Modernity Spectrum.

When looking at a school system, ask additional questions to understand where the school falls on the Modernity Spectrum, such as:

- Does this school equip students to engage effectively with the wider world beyond their religious community?

- Do students learn skills that help them work, travel, or talk to people who believe differently?

- If the answer is no, the school is likely non-modern.

- If the answer is yes, the school is closer to the modern side of the Spectrum.

Home Education as Religious Education

In some religious communities, families choose to homeschool their children because they do not trust outside schools. They believe public or secular schools teach ideas that go against their faith. These families often think modern education will weaken their children's beliefs. Homeschooling gives them full control over what their children see and learn.

In the United States, many non-modern Christian families homeschool their children. They may use religious books that teach Bible stories as history. Some of these books say dinosaurs lived at the same time as people. These families often avoid science, evolution, or other ideas that do not match their faith.

Some ultra-Orthodox Jewish families in the U.S. also homeschool for religious reasons. They want their children to learn Torah, Hebrew, and traditional customs. They often avoid teaching English, literature written in English, world history, or technology. These families believe too much contact with the outside world will harm their values.

In some Islamic communities, home education is used when families think public schools are too secular. They may fear their children will stop praying, eat forbidden food, or make non-Muslim friends. Teaching at home helps keep children inside their religious life. It also limits their knowledge of the modern world.

Germany does not allow homeschooling, even for religious reasons. But some non-modern families have left Germany to homeschool in other countries. They say the schools force children to learn ideas that go against their beliefs. These families are often deeply non-modern and fear outside influence.

In parts of rural Pakistan and Afghanistan, families may keep girls at home and teach them only religious lessons. They believe it is not proper for girls to go to school with boys or learn secular subjects. These girls may study the Qur'an and learn how to be good wives and mothers. They are not taught science, math, or other modern topics.

In these cases, homeschooling is not just about teaching at home—it is about keeping children away from modern ideas. The goal is to protect faith by avoiding outside knowledge. These families live on the non-modern side of the Modernity Spectrum. Their children may grow up deeply faithful, but also unprepared for life in the larger world.

Schooling Limited up to Certain Ages for "Religious Reasons"

A general rule is this: if children are only allowed to go to school for a few years before being removed for religious reasons, the system is likely non-modern. These practices usually limit learning about the outside world. They keep children focused only on faith and traditional roles. To understand where such schooling falls on the Modernity Spectrum, ask:

- How long are children allowed to study?

- What subjects are they taught?

- Are they prepared to enter the wider world when they leave school?

- What choices do they have afterward?

If schooling ends early and modern subjects are not taught, the group is likely non-modern.

In some ultra-Orthodox Jewish communities in the United States and Israel, boys may stop learning secular subjects by age 12 or 13. After that, they study only religious texts like the Talmud. Girls often leave school after a basic education to prepare for marriage and family. These communities believe that higher secular education is not needed for their religious way of life.

In rural parts of Afghanistan, girls are often pulled out of school around age 10 or 11. Some are never allowed to attend at all. Families fear that education will lead girls away from traditional roles. They believe that girls should focus on religion, modesty, and marriage, not careers or college.

In Yemen and parts of Somalia, some children stop formal schooling at a young age to memorize the Qur'an. This is seen as a great honor and duty. But once they finish memorizing, they may not continue with math, science, or writing. The goal is to become good Muslims, not modern professionals.

Among some conservative Christian groups in the United States, girls may be homeschooled or pulled from school early. These families believe a woman's place is in the home, not in the workplace. They may teach girls only basic reading and homemaking skills. Higher education is viewed as unnecessary—or even dangerous.

In some communities in Ethiopia and Nigeria, both boys and girls leave school young to join religious roles. They may serve in monasteries, temples, or churches. This early exit from school is seen as a spiritual calling. But it also means they miss out on learning other skills that could help them live in today's world.

Non-modern communities that limit schooling believe this protects their faith and culture. They worry that if children stay in school too long, they may question their beliefs. They may choose a different path. These communities choose to limit education to keep children close to tradition.

Summary

Education looks very different in different religious communities. Some faith groups believe learning helps people understand God and the world. They support schools that teach both religious and modern subjects. These schools often prepare students for work, college, and life in many places.

Other groups are afraid that modern education will harm faith. They may teach only religious texts or pull children out of school early. Some families homeschool to avoid outside ideas. In some countries, girls are not allowed to go to school past a young age.

We saw that Catholic, Buddhist, Hindu, Anglican, and Islamic schools around the world teach religion in different ways. Some of these schools are modern. Others are non-modern. What matters most is what students are allowed to learn—and what they are not.

To figure out where a school falls on the Modernity Spectrum, we ask:

- What subjects are taught?

- Are students trained to live only in their faith world—or also in the wider world?

- Do they learn to ask questions and explore different ideas?

- How long are they allowed to stay in school?

The more a school limits learning, the more non-modern it is. The more a school prepares students for many diverse parts of life, the more modern it is.

Education is one of the clearest ways to see how a religious group relates to the modern world. Some groups welcome science, history, and new ideas. Others see modern education as a danger to their way of life. This choice shapes what their children know—and what they are allowed to become.

My aunt's worry about her grandchildren shows this struggle in real life. Her daughter and son-in-law were both highly educated. They went to modern schools and became successful adults. But when they joined a non-modern religious community, they chose a different path for their children.

Those children were sent to schools that teach only religious subjects. They learned very little math, science, or English. Now, my aunt wonders if they can ever live outside their small community. She wonders if they are truly prepared for the modern world—or only for the world of their faith.

This story shows why education matters so much. Modern schools open doors. Non-modern schools build walls. Both paths are built with care and love, but they lead to very different futures.

When we look at religious education through the Modernity Spectrum, we can better understand these choices. We can see the values behind them. And we can ask—what kind of world are these schools preparing children to live in?

CHAPTER EIGHT

MARKER 7: LANGUAGE

I work as a Jewish chaplain in New York City. One concern I often hear from hospital staff is about ultra-Orthodox Jewish men who do not speak or understand English. They speak Yiddish as their primary—and sometimes only—language. Staff, especially those who were immigrants themselves, were confused. Many had worked hard to learn English so they and their families could fit into American society. They couldn't understand how a group of native-born Americans had never learned English.

This language difference created challenges in the hospital. Some staff felt frustrated or even disrespected. The situation became more difficult because of how these

Jewish men practiced modesty. For example, they often avoided looking women in the eyes. Many female staff members felt this was rude or dismissive, even though it came from religious belief. Together, the language barrier and modesty rules sometimes led to resentment and a feeling of othering.

Language plays a key role in many religions. Sacred texts are often written in one language, while the daily language of the community is another. To help bridge this gap, many religious communities offer after-school or weekend language classes. When I was growing up, I went to Hebrew school twice a week. Some of my friends went three or four times. My Greek neighbors attended Greek school at their church to learn the language of their prayers and sacred texts.

By age 13, I was expected to read Hebrew and follow along in the synagogue. In this way, I could take part in my faith's rituals even if I didn't speak Hebrew as a daily language. The dual use of language—for daily life and for ritual—can tell us a lot about where a group falls on the Modernity Spectrum. Some communities try to blend sacred and everyday languages. Others work hard to keep them separate. The next part of this chapter will explore this in greater depth.

Written Language

Written language holds a special place in nearly every faith tradition. Sacred texts—such as the Tripitaka (Buddhist), the Qur'an (Islam), the Tanach (Jewish), the Bible/New Testament (Christian), and the Bhagavad Gita (Hindu)—are often preserved in their original languages. For many believers, learning to read these texts in their original form is seen as a religious duty and a sign of deep faith. This reverence for the original written language can be a marker of where a group falls on the Modernity Spectrum.

In Roman Catholicism, for many centuries, the Mass was only conducted in Latin, even for people who did not understand it. Latin was considered the holy language, and its use was believed to preserve the purity of worship. It was not until the Second Vatican Council in the 1960s that the Church allowed Mass to be celebrated in local languages. This marked a major shift toward the modern end of the Modernity Spectrum, as it prioritized accessibility and comprehension over tradition.

By contrast, the Latin Mass is still practiced today by some traditional Catholic groups. These groups resist modern reforms and insist on using Latin as a sign of religious authenticity. Their preference for the Latin Mass places them closer to the non-modern end of the Modernity Spectrum, valuing tradition and separation from broader culture.

In Judaism, Torah scrolls are handwritten in Biblical Hebrew by trained scribes. Even though many Jews today speak modern Hebrew or other languages like English or Russian, the Torah must be read in its original form. Conservative and Orthodox communities often maintain Hebrew as the language of worship, while Reform congregations may include English to help with understanding. The balance of original and local language can reflect where a Jewish community falls on the Modernity Spectrum.

Islam teaches that the Qur'an must be read and recited in Arabic, even by people who do not speak Arabic in daily life. For millions of Muslims around the world, this means learning Classical Arabic for religious purposes only. While modern translations in local languages are often used for study and understanding, only the Arabic text is considered the true Qur'an.

This is especially striking in countries with large Muslim populations where Arabic is not spoken as a daily language. In Indonesia, the world's most populous Muslim-majority country, people speak Bahasa Indonesia. In Pakistan, it is Urdu. In Bangladesh, it is Bengali. In Turkey, people speak Turkish.

Despite these differences, believers in all these countries learn Arabic to read the Qur'an. This shows a strong commitment to religious tradition and sacred language, which leans toward the non-modern end of the Modernity Spectrum. Many non-modern Muslim communities focus exclusively on the Arabic text, avoiding translations altogether. However, modern Muslim groups often try to blend reverence for the original language with the need for understanding, using translated study guides and commentaries to help believers connect more deeply with their faith. This blending shows how language can reveal where a person or community falls on the Modernity Spectrum—whether they lean toward strict tradition or engage with both past and present.

Similarly, in Eastern Orthodox Christianity, liturgies are often conducted in Church Slavonic or ancient Greek. Some churches have transitioned to modern Russian or Greek, while others maintain the traditional forms. These choices affect how inclusive or separate a community feels and indicate their placement on the Modernity Spectrum.

In Hinduism, many sacred texts such as the Vedas are written in Sanskrit. Few Hindus today speak Sanskrit, but priests and scholars study and chant these texts in the original language. Some modern Hindu groups promote translations or simplified versions of these texts, which reflects a more modern approach to accessibility.

Buddhist scriptures, especially in Theravāda traditions, are preserved in Pāli. While monks may learn to read and chant in Pāli, lay practitioners are more likely to encounter the teachings in their own language. In modern Buddhist movements, translations are widely used, suggesting a shift toward the modern end of the Modernity Spectrum.

The role of written sacred language is complex. For some, it preserves the holiness and exactness of scripture. For others, it creates a barrier between faith and understanding. Where a group stands on these issues helps us understand how they balance tradition and accessibility.

Spoken Language

Spoken language is often more fluid than written language, but it too can be a sign of modernity or non-modernity in religious communities. The language people use every day reflects how much they interact with the modern world or how much they seek to remain separate.

For example, Amish and Old Order Mennonite communities in Pennsylvania and Ohio speak Pennsylvania Dutch, a dialect of German. They use language to maintain group identity and protect their community from outside influence. These communities teach English only for practical needs but prefer their traditional language in daily life.

In ultra-Orthodox Jewish communities in the United States, especially in Brooklyn or Monsey, New York, many people speak Yiddish as their main language. Children are raised speaking Yiddish at home and in school. Like the Amish and Old Order Mennonite communities who speak Pennsylvania Dutch, they use language to maintain group identity and protect their community from outside influence. English is taught only as a second language, if at all. This choice creates a clear cultural boundary and signals a desire to stay separate from the wider English-speaking society.

In contrast, most modern faith communities adopt the local or national language as their main spoken language. Evangelical churches in Latin America use Spanish or Portuguese. Buddhist temples in California use English for sermons and meditation classes. Muslim youth in France or Canada often speak the national language fluently and use it in religious settings alongside Arabic.

Language choices in worship also reflect modernity. In modern Christian churches, sermons and hymns are delivered in the local language. Contemporary churches use everyday speech to make religious ideas more understandable and relatable. This shift from formal or archaic language to modern spoken language often reflects a community's openness to change.

In some immigrant communities, language becomes a bridge. Korean churches in Los Angeles, for example, offer services in both Korean and English to include older members and second-generation youth. This blending of languages is a modern approach, aiming to include everyone.

Meanwhile, in traditional Buddhist monasteries in Thailand or Sri Lanka, monks may chant in Pāli but teach in the local language. This approach keeps the ancient language alive but also ensures that teachings are understood. It shows how communities can be both rooted and modern.

In Muslim communities around the world, especially outside the Arab world, spoken Arabic is often not used in daily life. While Arabic is still used for prayer and religious study, everyday conversations happen in local languages. To connect with younger generations, many religious leaders now use podcasts, videos, and social media in these national languages. This blending of traditional teachings with modern communication tools is a strong marker of modernity.

Overall, spoken language offers important clues about how a religious group relates to the broader world:

- Do they speak the common language?

- Do they use modern tools to communicate their faith?

- Or do they preserve a separate language to maintain boundaries?

The answers help place them on the Modernity Spectrum.

Chapter Nine

Marker 8: Food and Drink

Over the years I have been a rabbi, I have attended many multi-faith clergy meetings. A few times, different groups decided to share meals together. The goal each time was to build friendship and understanding. Everyone was asked to bring a dish that others could eat. We agreed on only vegetarian food—appetizers, main dishes, or desserts. This was an intentional act to include many of the clergy who often are not able to participate. This decision allowed Buddhist, Hindu, Muslim, and Jewish clergy to attend. Sharing the meal helped us feel close. Sitting together and eating together helped build trust. "Breaking bread" is one way to stop othering in religion. It is not always easy, but it can be done.

One of the best events I attended was a multi-national, multi-religious chaplains conference. To make everyone feel welcome, the planners made sure all main meals were kosher/halal (yes, this is possible but very rarely done). This way, everyone could eat together. No one had to sit alone. Vegetarian options were also included. These choices cost more, but they helped all chaplains attending, no matter what their faith tradition, feel respected. For many who often feel left out at meals, this was a big deal. It showed that everyone mattered.

I have another story, too. I went to a disaster training for chaplains in Arkansas. A group of us decided to eat together. A reservation was made. But the people who picked the restaurant didn't check for vegetarian options. When we got there, I found nothing I could eat. All the salads had bacon. The grill used lard, so no hot food was okay. I keep kosher, and one of my colleagues is a vegetarian for religious reasons. We had to leave and find food somewhere else. It felt awkward. It felt like we didn't belong.

Food rules can also show where someone falls on the Modernity Spectrum. Just as some faith communities use language, clothing, and even where they live to stay separate from modern society, strict food laws can serve the same purpose. For many non-modern groups, food is yet another line they draw to protect their way of life from outside influence. Kosher and halal laws, for example, dictate what foods can be eaten and how they must be prepared. These rules not only shape individual behavior but also create strong group boundaries.

Other groups take a more flexible approach. They may follow some food restrictions but find ways to eat with those who do not share their faith. In many cultures, sharing a meal is an important way to build relationships, but food restrictions can sometimes create barriers between different groups. Whether a person brings their own food, eats only what is "safe," or sits out entirely can signal where they fall on the Modernity Spectrum.

Religious Dietary Laws – Including Halal, Kosher, Vegetarianism, and Restrictions on Caffeine, Alcohol, Meat, and Other Forbidden Items

Many religions have food laws. These laws tell people what they can and cannot eat. They also say how food should be made. Some rules are very strict. Others are more flexible.

- **Buddhists** in some countries avoid meat. They believe in non-violence. Some eat fish or chicken, but not red meat. Monks in Thailand often eat only once a day. They take whatever food is offered.

- **Hindus** often do not eat beef. The cow is a holy animal. Some Hindus are also vegetarian. They believe it is wrong to harm animals. In India, many schools and temples serve only vegetarian food.

- **Muslims** follow halal rules. Alcohol is also forbidden. Meat must be killed in a certain way. Many Muslims read food labels to check for forbidden items.

- **Jews** who follow kosher rules eat only land animals that do not have split hooves and do not chew their cud. Like halal rules in Islam, kosher laws forbid pork. Shellfish and many other sea animals are also not allowed. Meat and milk cannot be mixed. Animals must be killed in a special way. Some Jews follow all the rules. Some follow only a few.

- **Latter-Day Saints** (Mormons) do not drink alcohol or coffee. They believe these drinks are harmful. They also avoid tea with caffeine. Many also avoid tobacco. Their faith teaches the body is a gift from God.

- **Seventh-Day Adventists** are often vegetarian. They avoid meat and alcohol. Many also avoid spicy food and caffeine. They believe food should help the body stay healthy and strong.

- **Rastafarians** follow a diet called "Ital." They eat natural, clean food. They avoid meat, salt, and anything with chemicals. Many are vegetarian or vegan. Their diet connects them to God and nature.

- Other religious groups have special fasting days or periods. For example,

  - **Eastern Orthodox Christians** fast from meat and dairy during Lent.

  - **Muslims** fast from dawn to sunset during Ramadan.

  - **Jews** fast on Yom Kippur and Tisha B'Av.

The Modernity Spectrum and Dietary Law

Food laws are not just about what people eat. They are also about how people live, what they believe, and how closely they hold onto tradition. These food choices—what is allowed or forbidden, what is shared or kept separate—can show where someone or a group falls on the Modernity Spectrum. Groups that strictly follow religious food rules often fall on the non-modern end of the Spectrum. Those that are more flexible in practice tend to fall on the modern end. These patterns often match other choices in life—such as language, dress, modesty, and whether someone sees their religion as one among many ("a faith") or as the one true path ("the faith").

Modern Hindus, for example, may avoid beef but still eat other meats like chicken or fish, especially outside the home. Some may switch between vegetarian and non-vegetarian eating depending on their setting or company. These choices reflect a modern mindset—honoring tradition while adapting to modern life. This flexibility often matches other modern traits: they might dress in both traditional Indian clothing and Western styles, speak English at work and Hindi or Tamil at home, and move easily between religious and secular worlds.

By contrast, non-modern Buddhists may follow strict rules about what they eat and when. Some only eat one meal a day, often before noon. Others avoid meat entirely and eat only food that is grown or prepared within their religious communities. This strong discipline often comes with other non-modern traits: simple dress, use of sacred languages in worship, gender-based roles, and a worldview that holds tightly to long-standing traditions.

In the Latter-Day Saints community, modern members may avoid alcohol and caffeine but drink herbal teas or eat meat occasionally. Their focus may be on health and spiritual balance, not strict rule-following. More non-modern Mormons, on the other hand, may follow every food rule closely—just as they may dress conservatively, live in close-knit religious communities, and avoid media or culture that conflicts with their beliefs. Their dietary rules are part of a wider commitment to live apart from secular culture.

Vegetarianism, as a faith practice, can exist across the Modernity Spectrum. Some follow it out of deep, non-negotiable religious belief, such as many Jains or strict Hindus. Others adopt it more flexibly, such as Buddhist monks who eat what is offered or clergy in multi-faith gatherings who choose vegetarian food to be inclusive. In these cases, the same practice (vegetarianism) can reflect very different places on the Modernity Spectrum, depending on the intention and degree of flexibility.

Strict halal Muslims are also generally on the non-modern side of the Spectrum. They eat only food that is halal certified, avoid any restaurant that serves pork or alcohol, and sometimes even bring their own food when visiting others. These food choices often align with other non-modern practices like wearing traditional modest dress, praying in Arabic, and maintaining theological boundaries between Islam and other faiths. Modern Muslims, in contrast, may still check food labels or avoid pork but feel comfortable eating vegetarian food at restaurants or accepting non-halal meat when no other options are available. Their flexibility with food often matches a broader approach to balancing religious identity and modern life.

Ultra-Orthodox Jews who observe all kosher rules also lean heavily toward the non-modern side. They eat only food that has been prepared under strict rabbinic supervision, avoid mixing milk and meat, and usually do not eat at restaurants or in homes that do not follow the same rules. These practices mirror their choices in other areas: they speak Yiddish, wear traditional clothing, practice strict gender separation, and see Judaism not just as a religion but as a full way of life. More modern

Jews may still honor kosher values but adjust in practical ways—like eating vegetarian in restaurants or choosing only certain kosher practices. These decisions reflect an effort to stay rooted in tradition while living fully in the modern world.

The Modernity Spectrum helps us understand how food laws—like language, dress, and modesty—can serve as both bridges and barriers. For non-modern communities, these rules protect the sacred and build internal strength by setting clear boundaries. For modern communities, food practices often support both identity and inclusion. They adapt tradition in ways that maintain meaning while allowing for connection with others.

Even something as simple as what someone eats—or refuses to eat—tells a big story. It reflects not just dietary preference, but deeper ideas about faith, belonging, identity, and how a community sees itself in relation to the modern world. When we take the time to understand these choices, we can reduce othering and open the door to shared meals, shared stories, and greater respect across all faiths.

Summary

Sharing food can build trust, respect, and belonging across faiths—as I've seen firsthand in my work as a rabbi. At multi-faith clergy gatherings, we chose vegetarian meals so everyone, including Buddhist, Hindu, Muslim, and Jewish leaders, could fully participate. At a global chaplains conference, serving meals that were both kosher and halal allowed everyone to sit together without worry. But at a chaplain training in Arkansas, a restaurant with no vegetarian or kosher options left two of us unable to eat—and feeling excluded. These moments show how food can either unite or divide. Dietary laws like kosher, halal, vegetarianism, or fasting often reflect how closely a person follows tradition. Some faith groups are strict, placing them on the non-modern side of the Modernity Spectrum. Others adapt their food practices to modern life, finding ways to stay connected while also being flexible.

Chapter Ten

Marker 9: Treatment of Women

This chapter and the next on Sex, Gender, and Sexuality have required the deepest thought and reflection. These two chapters explore some of the most sensitive, controversial, and emotionally intense topics in this book. I approached them with care, knowing how deeply these issues matter to many people of faith.

The treatment of women as it relates to religious people embracing or resisting the modern world is controversial. This topic is often heatedly debated. Further, it is one of the most talked-about topics in religion today. One issue is that there is often neither a common language nor taxonomy to frame the conversation so that it is less heated and becomes part of a larger discussion. Many people have very different views. Sometimes, people use different words or ideas,

To talk about this in a helpful way, we need a clear system. That system is the Modernity Spectrum. It helps us understand how religious people either accept or resist changes in the modern world. This chapter will look at how the treatment of women fits on the Modernity Spectrum. Sadly, most people do not use a shared framework like this. That makes true dialogue difficult.

The treatment of women is just one part of the Modernity Spectrum. It is not the only one. But it is one of the most visible signs of how modern or non-modern a faith group or individuals of faith may be.

Different faith traditions have varying roles for women. Some allow full participation in religious life, including leadership roles. Women can serve as clergy, lead prayers, and make religious decisions. Others limit women's roles, restricting them from leadership or requiring them to follow strict gender roles.

Some traditions encourage women to seek education and careers. Others expect them to focus on family and home life. The way a religious group treats women can tell us a lot about where they fall on the Modernity Spectrum. Groups that allow equal participation tend to fall on the modern end, while those that limit women's roles tend to be more non-modern.

Traditional Religious Views on the Roles of Women

The word "traditional" means something that has been done the same way for a long time. In religion, traditional often refers to beliefs or practices passed down from one generation to the next. These traditions may come from holy books, religious leaders, or customs that have lasted for hundreds or even thousands of years. People who follow traditional religion usually try to keep things the way they were in the past.

When we talk about traditional roles for women, we mean the way women have been expected to live and act in many religious communities over time. These roles are often linked to older ways of thinking and living. They are usually found in faith communities that are more non-modern on the Modernity Spectrum. These communities often see these roles as sacred, not just cultural.

In Christianity, the New Testament includes passages such as 1 Timothy 2:12, which says, "I do not permit a woman to teach or to assume authority over a man; she must be quiet." In many of the more non-modern "traditional" Christian denominations, this has been interpreted to mean that women should not serve as clergy or hold leadership roles in the church. The Virgin Mary is often upheld as the ideal woman: humble, obedient, and faithful. Many Christian communities continue to view a woman's highest calling as being a wife and mother.

In Islam, the Quran and Hadith (sayings of the Prophet Muhammad) provide guidance on gender roles. Surat An-Nisā in The Quran (4:34) describes men as "protectors and maintainers of women." Classical Islamic law often placed women under the guardianship of male relatives. Traditional roles emphasize the woman's responsibilities in childbearing, raising children, and managing the home. Modesty and obedience are frequently emphasized, with women often discouraged from leadership roles in public or religious settings. However, Islamic scholars vastly differ on the implications of this verse, with many Muslim scholars saying that it serves as a deterrent from anger-based domestic violence.

Buddhism also reflects traditional gender roles in many of its sects. While the Buddha allowed women to become nuns, their status was usually considered subordinate to that of monks. In many traditions, women must follow more rules than men to be ordained. Teachings often stress rebirth as a man as more favorable, reinforcing the idea that male birth is spiritually advantageous.

In Confucian-influenced societies such as China and Korea, traditional values have long emphasized a strict gender hierarchy. The "Three Obediences" (to father, husband, and son) outlined a woman's expected subservience at every stage of life. Confucianism promotes harmony and hierarchy within the family, with the male as the head and the woman as caretaker and moral guide within the home.

In Judaism, traditional texts like the Tanach and later commentaries such as the Talmud outline specific roles for women. The Tanach praises women for their roles as mothers, wives, and keepers of the home. Proverbs 31 describes the "Eshet Chayil," or "Woman of Valor," who is industrious, modest, and devoted to her family.

Rabbinic writings often are interpreted to limit public leadership roles for women while placing high value on modesty, child-rearing, and home-making.

In Hinduism, ancient texts such as the Manusmriti and the Dharmashastras describe women as dependent on their fathers, husbands, and sons at different stages of life. The ideal woman is loyal, obedient, and devoted to her family. The concept of "stridharma" (women's dharma or duty) emphasizes roles within the household, often placing women in a supportive and submissive role. Sita, a Hindu Goddess from the Ramayana, is a traditional model of wifely devotion and sacrifice.

Traditional indigenous religions across the world also contain gender-specific roles. In some African tribal religions, women are seen as life-givers and are central to fertility rites. Yet leadership in religious ceremonies is often male-dominated. In Native American cultures, roles varied by tribe, but many traditions had clear divisions of labor and authority based on gender.

These traditional roles are deeply woven into the structure of religious communities and practices. They are often reinforced through storytelling, religious schooling, and communal expectations. Women who follow these roles are praised for their piety, modesty, and devotion. Departure from these roles is sometimes met with criticism or social consequences.

Religious dress codes also stem from these traditional views. Modesty in clothing often symbolizes a woman's commitment to religious values. This includes head coverings for Muslim women (hijab), married Orthodox Jewish women (tichel or sheitel), and Christian women in certain denominations. Modest dress is seen not only as obedience to God but also as a marker of community identity.

Childbearing and child-rearing are central to many traditional religious views of womanhood. Women are often told that motherhood is their sacred duty. Religious rituals, such as naming ceremonies, coming-of-age rituals, and family prayers, often highlight the woman's role as the heart of the household and the transmitter of faith.

In many traditional communities, the ideal woman is both visible and invisible—seen in her faithful actions but often unheard in public life. She supports her husband, raises children in the faith, and maintains the household. Leadership, public voice, and religious authority are often reserved for men.

These traditional roles are not simply outdated ideas; they remain active in many religious communities around the world. They are often justified as timeless truths handed down from God or divine order. For communities on the non-modern end of the Modernity Spectrum, preserving these roles is seen as preserving the faith itself.

Understanding these traditional views is essential to grasping why changes in the role of women are so controversial in some faith communities. The more closely a group adheres to these traditional teachings, the more likely they are to resist modern ideas about gender equality. As we will explore in the next section, some communities are reinterpreting these traditions, while others stand firmly against change.

How Modern Faith Communities Have Reinterpreted Women's Roles

Many faith communities have changed how they see the roles of women. These changes reflect a move along the Modernity Spectrum. Groups that once restricted women are now giving them new opportunities to learn, lead, and teach. These changes often happen slowly and are shaped by culture, geography, and local values.

In Protestant Christianity, many churches now ordain women as ministers or priests. The Anglican Church has women bishops in some countries. The United Methodist Church and the Evangelical Lutheran Church in America both have women in top leadership. These shifts reflect modernity in their view of women and leadership.

In contrast, the Roman Catholic Church does not ordain women as priests. However, Roman Catholic women now lead major church organizations, teach theology, and serve as spiritual directors. The majority of Board Certified Roman Catholic Chaplains are women. Some groups are pushing for more change, while others want to keep tradition. This mix shows the tension between modern and non-modern positions.

In Islam, some modern communities are exploring new roles for women. In the U.S. and Europe, there are now women-led mosques. One of the first, the Women's Mosque of America, opened in Los Angeles in 2015. In these spaces, women lead prayers, give sermons, and run programs. The Women's Mosque of America had precedents in other countries in Muslim-majority nations and elsewhere. Further, women have taken leadership roles in the field of professional chaplaincy in the U.S. These are new ideas in many Muslim cultures and reflect a modern approach.

In more conservative Muslim communities, women still face limits. They may not lead prayers or speak in public religious settings. Still, many women are becoming scholars, teachers, and leaders of women's religious circles. They publish books and give lectures. Some communities accept these roles as ways to stay faithful while engaging the modern world.

In Judaism, the Reform and Conservative movements began ordaining women as rabbis in the late 20th century. The first female rabbi in the U.S., Sally Priesand, was ordained in 1972. Today, many Reform and Conservative synagogues have female rabbis, cantors, and leaders. These communities are more modern on the Modernity Spectrum.

In Orthodox Judaism, change has come more slowly. Some women both in Israel and the U.S., are now being trained as halakhic (Jewish law) advisors or spiritual leaders. Although not called "rabbis," they teach, preach, and answer questions about Jewish law. Some Orthodox communities see this as a step toward greater inclusion. Others strongly resist it, staying more firmly non-modern.

In Hinduism, change has also come. Women now study at seminaries and become spiritual teachers. In India and abroad, female gurus lead large communities. Amma (Mata Amritanandamayi), known for hugging thousands of people in blessing, is one famous example. Women can also perform rituals and serve in temple leadership in many modern Hindu groups.

In Buddhism, especially in the West, many women are now fully ordained as nuns and spiritual teachers. Some Buddhist centers are led by women. In countries like Thailand and Myanmar, full ordination for women is still debated, but women's access to teaching and meditation leadership has grown.

Education is another key area of change. In many parts of the world, girls were once denied religious education. Today, modern communities are making sure girls learn to read sacred texts and study religious history. In Muslim-majority countries, female Quran scholars are becoming more visible. In modern Jewish communities, girls attend the same religious schools as boys.

These changes often come with tension. Some members want to keep the old ways. Others want to grow and change. This tension is a normal part of the Modernity Spectrum. Each community moves at its own pace, shaped by its beliefs, leadership, and history.

What connects all these stories is a shift in how faith is practiced. When women are allowed to learn, lead, and speak, their communities often become more open. These are signs of moving toward modernity. But each change must still fit within the values of the faith tradition.

By looking at these shifts, we see how modernity reshapes the lives of religious women. It does not mean losing faith—it means living it differently. Women are reinterpreting their roles in ways that reflect both tradition and the world they live in today.

The Powerful Impact of the Modernity Spectrum on Women's Lives

Where a faith community falls on the Modernity Spectrum shapes nearly every part of women's lives. It affects their role in religious life, their chances for education, their place in the family, and even their ability to earn money. Often, these shifts are the most visible signs of how a community is changing—or staying the same.

In non-modern communities, women are often expected to follow strict rules. They may not be allowed to lead prayer, read sacred texts in public, or study religious law. Family roles in non-modern communities are often clearly defined. Women are expected to marry young, have many children, and take care of the home. In some Hindu and Christian groups, this is seen as part of a woman's sacred duty. Her value is tied to her family role. She may have few choices outside of this path.

As faith communities become more modern many of the above patterns begin to shift. Religious leadership begins to open. In modern Protestant churches, women may lead congregations and serve as bishops. In Buddhist centers in the U.S. and Europe, women lead meditation retreats and teach the Dharma. In modern Jewish communities, women read from the Torah, give sermons, and become rabbis.

Family expectations change as well. In modern communities, women may choose when or if they marry. They may have fewer children, and parenting is often shared with their partner. Birth control is accepted, and reproductive choices are made by the couple, not the community.

These changes can be very controversial. Some people fear that opening women's roles will weaken the community's identity. Others see these changes as signs of growth and health. For example, when women are given education and leadership roles, faith communities often thrive and grow stronger.

Even small changes can make a big difference. Allowing women to lead prayer at a women's gathering or read a sacred text aloud may spark hope—or debate. These steps are often the first signs of movement on the Modernity Spectrum. Modern women within non-modern communities also face challenges. They may want more freedom, but still deeply love their tradition. Some create new spaces—like all-women prayer groups—to balance faith and change. Others leave their communities to seek new forms of spiritual life.

Social media has played a large role in this. Women now share stories, support one another, and challenge old rules online. They build networks that cross borders, traditions and even religions. This global conversation is helping more women question where their community stands on the Modernity Spectrum—and where they want it to go.

The impact of the Modernity Spectrum on women's lives is deep and wide. It touches prayer, education, family, dress, and identity. For many women, it defines what is possible in both faith and life. Understanding this helps us see why these changes matter so much—and why they are sometimes met with resistance.

When we look at how a community treats its women, we learn a lot about how it sees itself.

- Is it open to change?

- Or is it trying to hold on tightly to the past?

The answers to these questions tell us where a group falls on the Modernity Spectrum—and how women live as a result.

Marriage, Family, and Reproductive Roles

Marriage and family life are central parts of most religious traditions. In many faiths, these areas carry deep religious meaning and are guided by sacred texts and long-held customs. These teachings often include ideas about who should marry, when, how many children to have, and the specific roles of husbands and wives.

In non-modern religious communities, marriage is often seen as a duty, not just a personal choice. Marriage may happen early in life, and having children is usually expected. In some communities, women may be matched with a partner by family or religious leaders. Their role as a wife and mother is seen as a sacred responsibility.

For example, in some ultra-Orthodox Jewish communities, matchmaking (called shidduchim) is done by family and community members. Women may marry as teenagers and are expected to have large families.

Birth control is rarely discussed and may be discouraged. Similarly, in many conservative Muslim communities, women are expected to marry early and prioritize raising children.

In traditional Hindu communities, arranged marriage is still common, especially in rural areas. Women may have limited say in who they marry. The idea of dharma (sacred duty) includes caring for the household, husband, and children. Having sons may be especially valued for spiritual and social reasons.

Catholic teaching also emphasizes marriage as a sacred union, open to having children. The Catholic Church traditionally opposes birth control, although many modern Catholic couples make their own choices. In some more non-modern Catholic communities, families remain large, and gender roles are clearly divided.

Among Evangelical Christians, family life is often taught as a woman's highest calling. Women are encouraged to marry, raise children, and support their husband's leadership. In non-modern Evangelical groups, women may be discouraged from working outside the home or seeking leadership roles.

In contrast, modern faith communities often give women more freedom in marriage and family decisions. Marriage may happen later in life. Couples may choose whether to have children. Women may delay or avoid pregnancy using birth control, which is often accepted or quietly practiced.

Modern Buddhist women, for example, may marry or remain single. They may choose to have children or live as nuns. The choice is personal, not a religious requirement. In urban Hindu families, arranged marriages still happen, but many women now meet partners through school, work, or online platforms.

In modern Muslim communities in places like Indonesia, Turkey, or the United States, women often choose when and whom to marry. Birth control is more widely accepted, and many women work outside the home. These changes reflect a more modern stance on the Modernity Spectrum.

Some faith traditions now bless same-sex marriages. In Reform Judaism, the United Church of Christ, and some branches of Buddhism and Unitarian Universalism, marriage is seen as a commitment between loving partners—not limited to a man and a woman. These changes also signal a move toward the modern end of the Modernity Spectrum.

Reproductive roles are among the most emotionally charged topics. In non-modern groups, women may not be allowed to choose if or when to have children. Birth control, abortion, or fertility treatments may be forbidden. These restrictions are often based on religious texts or teachings about life and the soul.

In contrast, modern groups often support women's access to reproductive health care. They may bless adoption, support family planning, and make space for women who choose not to have children. In some traditions, these changes are part of a larger shift toward personal freedom and gender equality.

The Modernity Spectrum helps us see how deeply religious views about marriage and family shape women's lives. Communities that stay near the non-modern end tend to hold onto traditional views. Those that move toward the modern end often rethink gender roles, family size, and women's choices. These changes are not always easy. They can create tension within families and religious groups. But they are also signs of growth, agency, and deep spiritual reflection.

How Women Themselves Locate Their Faith and Identity on the Modernity Spectrum

The Modernity Spectrum is not just something we use to describe religious communities from the outside. Many women within those communities also use it, unconsciously and not knowingly, to make sense of their lives, their roles, and their faith journeys. Some women embrace non-modern communities with deep pride. Others seek change, either from within their tradition or by stepping outside of it. Women's voices in these settings show that where one stands on the Modernity Spectrum is not just about doctrine—it's about identity, agency, and belonging.

For many women in non-modern communities, traditional roles are a source of strength. They may feel honored by religious texts that define women as nurturers, caregivers, or keepers of the home. These women often describe their lives as spiritually rich and anchored by faith. Others in similar settings feel confined. They may love their faith but feel frustrated by the limited roles available to them. Some women in these communities begin to challenge the boundaries from within.

In many African Christian communities, women have traditionally been expected to focus on domestic responsibilities and support roles within the church. Patriarchal cultural norms often reinforce these expectations, limiting women's opportunities for theological education and leadership.

However, African women theologians, such as Mercy Amba Oduyoye and Esther Mombo, have been instrumental in challenging these traditional roles. Oduyoye founded the Circle of Concerned African Women Theologians to promote women's theological scholarship and leadership. Mombo has advocated for women's ordination and addressed issues of gender-based violence within the church. Their work represents a significant shift towards greater inclusion of women in African Christian communities.

Muslim feminists offer another powerful example. In countries like Malaysia, Indonesia, and the United States, women scholars are rereading the Qur'an with fresh eyes. They argue that many restrictions placed on women stem not from the text itself but from centuries of male-dominated interpretation. Some have launched women-led mosques or taken on leadership in interfaith and academic settings. These women often live between the traditional and the modern, embracing faith while insisting it evolve.

Some women leave their communities entirely when change seems impossible. Former Mormon or Hasidic women, for example, sometimes share stories of feeling silenced or ignored. For them, exiting the community is a painful but empowering decision. They may retain aspects of faith but reject the structures that once confined them. These women often find support in online forums, memoirs, or advocacy work. Their journeys show that moving along the Modernity Spectrum isn't always a communal shift—sometimes it's personal.

Still, not every woman sees modernity as progress. Some who leave modern religious settings return to more traditional communities seeking order, clarity, and connection. They may tire of the ambiguity in modern theology or feel disconnected from secular culture. These women may embrace modest dress, structured prayer, or defined gender roles not as limitations but as forms of liberation. For them, the Modernity Spectrum is not a ladder to climb—it's a compass to navigate, with different values at each point.

Importantly, women's positions on the Modernity Spectrum are not fixed. A woman may move toward tradition during child-rearing years, then later embrace modern views. Others may adopt modern education but maintain non-modern dress or food practices. Faith is dynamic, and so are the women who live it. They are not passive followers—they are interpreters, challengers, and keepers of their traditions.

In every faith, women are asking: "Where do I stand?" and "Where do I want to go?" The Modernity Spectrum offers a helpful way to frame these questions, but it doesn't decide the answers. Women do.

Their stories—of staying, changing, questioning, and leading—remind us that faith and identity are not one-size-fits-all. The Modernity Spectrum is a tool, not a judgment. And women's voices are central to understanding how that tool is used, stretched, and sometimes even redefined.

Summary

This chapter has explored how different faith communities treat women and how those views connect to the Modernity Spectrum. We looked at traditional roles for women, how those roles are changing, and the deep impact these changes have on women's lives. We also listened to women's voices and how they see their own faith and identity. Finally, we explored how marriage, family, and reproductive choices are shaped by where a community stands on the Modernity Spectrum.

In many non-modern communities, women are expected to follow strict gender roles, often based on ancient texts and customs. In more modern communities, women are finding new ways to live their faith while also embracing education, leadership, and personal choice. These changes do not always happen easily. They come with conflict, debate, and sometimes pain. But they also bring new hope and possibilities.

Understanding where a community stands on the Modernity Spectrum helps us talk more clearly and respectfully about these issues. It gives us a shared language to explore difficult topics. And most of all, it reminds us that every woman's experience deserves to be seen and honored, no matter where she stands on the Modernity Spectrum.

CHAPTER ELEVEN

MARKER 10: SEX, GENDER, AND SEXUALITY

This chapter and the previous one on "Treatment of Women" have required the deepest thought and reflection. These two chapters explore some of the most sensitive, controversial, and emotionally intense topics in this book. I approached them with care, knowing how deeply these issues matter to many people of faith.

Introduction

Growing up, I spent my summers at Jewish camps that were fully kosher and strictly observed Shabbat. One of the phrases I heard from a very young age—third or fourth grade—was, "It's a double mitzvah on Shabbat."

This referred to sex between married couples being not just permitted, but sacred on the Sabbath. It was said plainly, almost casually. No shame. No secrecy.

It wasn't until high school that I realized this openness was not universal. At my public school, I mentioned that sex was talked about openly at Jewish summer camp. One classmate who had attended a Christian camp was shocked. "They talked about that at camp? That would never happen where I went."

In nearly every Jewish community—no matter where they fall on the Modernity Spectrum—this idea that sex is not bad, but sacred, is familiar. But while the phrase may be widely known, actual conversations about sex, gender, and sexuality are often avoided or highly restricted as people get older. This is not just a Jewish phenomenon—it is true across most religions.

Religious traditions around the world hold powerful beliefs about sex, gender, and sexuality. These beliefs shape how people live, love, marry, and see themselves. Some embrace modern understandings; others resist them. Where a community stands on these topics is one of the clearest ways to see where they fall on the Modernity Spectrum.

Overview

Religions and people of faith have different beliefs about sex, gender, and sexuality. What a person of faith believes about sex, gender, and sexuality can often shape how and who they connect with in the world of today.

One reason the Modernity Spectrum has many elements on it is that someone might fall into the modern end of the Spectrum regarding science, technology, language, physical or social isolation. However, their views regarding sex, gender, and sexuality may fall elsewhere on the Spectrum. People of faith often have views in different areas of the Modernity Spectrum that fall in different places along the Spectrum.

Some people of faith believe that one should not have sex until they are married. They believe sex should only happen inside marriage. Other people of faith, even within the same religion, may have a different view. They think sexuality is a personal choice. They believe love and commitment are more important than a "traditional" marriage. Some people of faith believe that a man can and should have multiple wives. Other people of faith within the same religion strongly believe the opposite.

Some people of faith strongly believe there are only two genders: male and female. They think these roles are given by God and should not change. They expect men and women to act in certain ways and do certain jobs. These beliefs affect family life, work, and how people live in their communities.

Other people of faith accept non-binary people and include LGBTQ+ people. They believe gender is more complex. They turn to science and scientific understandings to help shape their beliefs. They think faith should support everyone, no matter their gender identity.

The Modernity Spectrum and Identity Tensions

Not all people or faith groups think the same about sex, gender, and sexuality. Some stay close to old rules. Others accept new ideas. This is where the Modernity Spectrum helps. It shows how much a group accepts or resists the modern world.

A community may be modern in some ways—like using science, smartphones, or modern medicine—but non-modern in others. Sex and gender are often the areas where people are most resistant to change. Even when someone uses the internet every day, they may still believe very old ideas about gender roles or who someone can love.

For example, some Christian groups now welcome LGBTQ+ people and perform same-sex weddings. They believe their faith calls them to love and include everyone. But other Christian groups say the Bible only allows marriage between a man and a woman. They believe God made only two genders. These groups are on different parts of the Modernity Spectrum.

In Judaism, as you saw earlier, some communities allow LGBTQ+ Jews to become rabbis and get married in the synagogue. Others do not. The same is true in Islam. Some Muslim communities support queer Muslims and their families. Others say being gay or trans is wrong. These beliefs shape how people live and whether they feel safe in their own faith.

In India, Hijras have been part of Hindu life for centuries. They are gender-diverse people who often bless weddings and births. In some places they are honored. In other places, they are pushed away. This shows a tension between traditional respect and modern rejection. It depends where a group sits on the Modernity Spectrum.

In Buddhism, especially in Thailand, kathoey people—who may be transgender women—have long been part of the culture. But in some modern Buddhist communities, they are not allowed to become monks. Some say this is the "ancient way," even though the past tells a different story.

Sometimes the fight over sex, gender, and sexuality becomes louder than other parts of religion. It becomes a line in the sand. People use it to decide who is "faithful" and who is not. This creates pain. It also creates tension inside families, communities, and religious groups.

When people move toward the non-modern side of the Modernity Spectrum in these areas, they often say they are "protecting tradition." But sometimes they are ignoring parts of that tradition that made space for more gender identities or kinds of love. They remember only some teachings and forget the rest.

At the same time, those who move toward the modern side often use both tradition and science. They look back at old texts and stories and find new meaning. They also listen to doctors, psychologists, and others to understand more about human identity. They try to hold both their faith and today's knowledge.

People of faith live at many points along the Modernity Spectrum. Some move between points. Some change over time. Others stay in one place for a lifetime. The Modernity Spectrum helps us understand why that happens and how these tensions shape religious life.

What matters most is how we treat each other. Even when we disagree, the goal is to listen, to care, and to keep the conversation going. That is what makes faith strong—not silence, but compassion.

Sacred Texts, Interpretation, and Authority

Many religious views on sex, gender, and sexuality come from sacred texts. But how people read those texts can be very different. Some read them literally—word for word—as unchanging truth. Others read them in context, asking what the text meant back then, and what it might mean today. Where a group stands on this issue often shows where they fall on the Modernity Spectrum.

In Christianity, the Bible is central. Some churches say same-sex relationships are sinful because of verses in Leviticus or Romans. They take these words literally. Other churches say those verses reflect a different time. They ask, "What was the cultural context?" and "What would Jesus say today?" These churches welcome LGBTQ+ people. They believe love and justice are more important than following rules without question.

In Judaism, the Tanach and Talmud are key. Some Orthodox groups say Jewish law never changes. They keep strict rules about gender roles and marriage. Other groups—like Reform and Conservative Jews—believe Jewish texts are living documents. They read them with modern eyes. They look for ways to stay faithful while being inclusive.

In Islam, the Qur'an is sacred. It speaks about modesty, marriage, and gender roles. Some Muslims say these rules must be followed exactly as written. Others study how Islamic law (sharia) developed over time. They find ways to honor the Qur'an while also supporting women's rights and LGBTQ+ dignity. Muslim scholars—especially women—are leading this work today.

In Hinduism and Buddhism, texts also shape beliefs. Some Hindus point to ancient stories to support gender roles. Others point to stories of gods with both male and female traits. Some Buddhists say the Buddha's teachings don't allow LGBTQ+ people to be monks. Others say the Buddha taught compassion and would include all.

In every tradition, there are people who use sacred texts to exclude—and people who use them to include. This is not just about the text itself. It's about how much a group is willing to engage with modern ideas, science, and lived experience. That's what moves them along the Modernity Spectrum.

Authority matters too. Who gets to decide what a text means? In some communities, only men—or only clergy—can speak. In others, women, laypeople, and LGBTQ+ voices are heard. In modern groups, authority is often shared. In non-modern groups, it may be tightly controlled.

Interpretation and authority go hand in hand. When one changes, the other often changes too. And those changes show us a lot about where a community is—and where it may be going.

Gender Diversity and Trans Inclusion

When I was in rabbinical school, we studied Jewish law in great detail. We learned how different religious obligations were assigned to men and women. For example, who is required to say certain prayers, or who lights the candles to welcome the Sabbath. Gender was more than just identity—it was central to how a person was expected to live a Jewish life. The ancient rabbis paid close attention to gender because it shaped legal responsibilities and community roles.

But here's something many people don't realize: Jewish tradition has long acknowledged that not everyone fits neatly into "male" or "female." The Talmud and later Jewish legal texts speak about individuals who live somewhere in between—or outside—those categories. This isn't modern innovation. It's ancient wisdom.

There are Hebrew terms for several gender-diverse identities. "Zachar" means male. "Nekeva" means female. But there are also terms like "androgynos," which refers to someone with both male and female physical traits—mentioned 149 times in the Mishnah and Talmud, and hundreds more in later rabbinic texts. "Tumtum" refers to someone whose sexual characteristics are hidden or indeterminate. There are also "ay'lonit," individuals assigned female at birth who develop male traits at puberty, and "saris," assigned male at birth but who develop female traits.

These categories are not marginal. They are part of mainstream Jewish law, found in the foundational texts that observant Jews study every day.

Yet, in many non-modern Jewish communities today—those who resist modernity in the area of sex and gender—these teachings are often forgotten or ignored. People act as if gender diversity is new, or "outside the tradition." But the tradition tells a different story.

This is a good example of how the Modernity Spectrum helps us understand religious life. Some groups resist science and modern social understandings around gender. But they also close their eyes to their own sources. They deny the complexity their tradition once recognized.

In contrast, more modern Jewish communities are recovering these ancient texts. They use them to support inclusion and respect for transgender and non-binary Jews. They are not inventing something new. They are reclaiming something old.

This pattern exists in other religions too. Non-modern groups often reject gender diversity as "modern," when their own traditions hold traces of it. This chapter will explore those tensions—and possibilities.

As both a rabbi and a person of faith, I find it powerful that Jewish tradition has made space for people with diverse gender identities for thousands of years. These ancient categories show that gender diversity is not a new idea—it is something our ancestors saw and made space for.

This pattern is not unique to Judaism. We can see the same thing happen in other world religions. In each case, traditions that once made space for gender complexity are now often claimed by non-modern communities as rigidly binary. As these communities resist modern understandings of gender, they often forget or erase the nuance that was once part of their own faith.

In Islam, the sacred texts and classical jurisprudence include discussions about "khuntha," often translated as "intersex" individuals. Islamic scholars, especially in medieval times, recognized the existence of people who could not be classified clearly as male or female. Classical Islamic law books offer legal guidance for how such individuals should pray, inherit property, and be treated in society. In some schools of Islamic law, there is even advice about surgical and social transition if a person's identity becomes clearer over time. Yet many non-modern Muslim communities today insist that Islam only recognizes two genders. As with Judaism, the deeper historical record shows a more layered reality—one that is often overlooked when communities place themselves firmly on the non-modern end of the Modernity Spectrum.

In Hindu traditions, the recognition of gender diversity goes back thousands of years. The Hijra community in South Asia—people who may be transgender, intersex, or non-binary—has a long cultural and spiritual history. In some Hindu texts, Hijras are seen as having special spiritual power. They are often called upon to offer blessings at weddings and births. The deity Shiva is sometimes portrayed as Ardhanarishvara—half male and half female—showing a divine balance of gender. Yet in modern-day India, Hijras often face legal and social exclusion, especially from more conservative, non-modern Hindu groups who view their identities as illegitimate or sinful. This disconnection between tradition and present-day practice shows how far a community can move away from its own roots in order to resist modernity.

Christianity also contains examples, though they are often hidden beneath layers of interpretation. Some early Christian texts describe followers who lived outside traditional gender roles. In the New Testament, there is mention of the Ethiopian eunuch—a gender-nonconforming person who is baptized and fully welcomed into the early Christian community. Later Christian history includes people who lived celibate lives in monastic settings, where gender norms were often blurred. Saints like Joan of Arc wore men's clothing and assumed male roles, which was seen at the time as both spiritual and radical. Today, however, many conservative Christian groups deny any space for non-binary or trans individuals. They position their views as "traditional," even when the historical record is more complex.

In Buddhism, especially in Southeast Asian contexts, there is a long-standing awareness of gender fluidity. In Thailand, for example, the term "kathoey" has been used for centuries to describe people who might today identify as transgender women or gender nonconforming. While the social position of kathoey people has varied over time, there is clear evidence of their cultural presence and participation in religious life. However, some non-modern Buddhist communities still exclude trans people from monastic orders or restrict their roles. They frame these exclusions as based in ancient teaching, despite historical records showing otherwise.

In each of these religious traditions, we see a similar tension: gender diversity has always existed. It was often recognized and, in some cases, respected. But when communities move farther into the non-modern end of the Modernity Spectrum—especially in matters of sex and gender—they often erase their own history. They frame their current rejection of gender diversity as "faithful," even when it contradicts their tradition's own sources.

More modern faith communities, by contrast, are often recovering these older voices and ideas. They draw on sacred texts, history, and science to build more inclusive spiritual spaces. They don't see this as abandoning their faith. They see it as fulfilling it—bringing ancient wisdom into dialogue with modern understanding.

This is one of the core insights of the Modernity Spectrum: many religious people aren't choosing between tradition and modernity. They are choosing how to hold both—how to stay faithful while also growing. Gender diversity and trans inclusion are two of the clearest places where we can see this struggle unfold.

Summary: Sex, Gender, and Sexuality

Sex, gender, and sexuality are among the most personal and emotionally charged areas of religious life. This chapter explored how faith communities interpret and respond to these topics, and how those responses often reflect where a group stands on the Modernity Spectrum.

Some religious groups hold to long-standing, binary views of gender and strict rules around sex and marriage. Others embrace more inclusive and complex understandings shaped by both sacred texts and modern knowledge. Interestingly, many non-modern groups that resist change in these areas often overlook parts of their own religious traditions that made space for gender diversity and sexual variation. This was seen in Judaism, Islam, Christianity, Hinduism, and Buddhism.

The Modernity Spectrum helps us understand these tensions. It shows how some people of faith are trying to hold both tradition and change—honoring the past while making room for new realities. Others retreat into more rigid interpretations, sometimes forgetting the full richness of their own history.

Ultimately, this chapter encourages compassion. People may disagree on these issues, but listening, empathy, and dialogue are what keep faith communities strong and open to growth.

Conclusion

A Truth versus The Truth – How Religious People Embrace or Resist the Modern World

This book introduced a framework called the Modernity Spectrum—a way to understand how religious people and communities respond to the modern world. Across topics like science, medicine, technology, education, gender, violence, clothing, food, and identity, we saw that faith communities often fall along different points on the Modernity Spectrum. Some embrace modernity fully. Others resist it strongly. Many live somewhere in between.

Each chapter showed how responses to modernity vary both between and within religious traditions. Importantly, a single person or group may be modern in some areas (like using smartphones or accepting science) and non-modern in others (like rejecting gender diversity or LGBTQ+ inclusion). The Modernity Spectrum makes room for this complexity. It helps us see patterns, tensions, and choices that are often hidden beneath surface-level beliefs.

By the end of the book, one truth becomes clear: modernity is not all-or-nothing. And neither is tradition. Most people of faith are trying to balance the two. They draw from sacred texts and ancient wisdom while also grappling with new realities and ethical questions.

The goal of this book was not to judge where someone is on the Modernity Spectrum. The goal was to help readers recognize where they—and others—stand, and to encourage honest, respectful conversation about why. Understanding these patterns can help build more compassionate communities, inside and outside religious life.

www.ingramcontent.com/pod-product-compliance
Lightning Source LLC
Chambersburg PA
CBHW070626030426
42337CB00020B/3932